Backyard Brighton

new memories, reflections and photographs

Brighton Books Publishing

TO
LET

Contents

Foreword 7
Introduction 9
Preface 17
Map 18
Cavendish Street 21
William Street 25
Nelson Street 30
Carlton Row 31
Albion Street 34
Henry Street 38
Nelson Place 39
Circus Street 41
Albion Cottages 42
Carlton Street 45
Mount Pleasant 47
Apollo Terrace 48
Ivory Place 51
Sussex Street 53
Oxford Court 57
Preece's Buildings 63
101 North Street 67
Russell Place 69
Sun Street 71
Gloucester Terrace 72
Park Place 79
Gerrard's Court 80
Carlton Hill 85
Edwin Place 86
Boss's Gardens 91
Hayllars Cottages 95
Artillery Street 97
End Piece 99
Afterword: Kingswood Flats 100
Interviews 103
Acknowledgements 104
Backlist 105

Cover: Sussex Street 1930s
Inside front cover: Dorset Buildings, 32 Edward Street to Carlton Hill 1930s
First page: doorway at Carlton Court, 9 Carlton Hill
Opposite title page: Hayllar's Cottages looking west 1935

Opposite: Lewis's Buildings at 36 Ship Street 1935

Foreword

I first heard of the collection of 'slum' photographs from an Environmental Health officer in the early 1980s. When I asked whether I could see them they admitted they had been lost. I asked about them several times over the next few years. Then, to my astonishment, I received a 'phone call to say that they had been found. What is more I was allowed to borrow them. They were handed to me in a paper carrier bag. I had no idea what I would find. It was a wonderful surprise when I discovered the outstanding and haunting quality of the photographs, a record of the buildings scheduled for demolition in the 1930s

The photographs were commissioned from the photographer Vawdrey of Dyke Road, Brighton, 'to demonstrate those features of unfitness upon which the cases for clearance were based, elements of disrepair, dampness, lighting, ventilation, sanitary arrangements and bad arrangement'.

The photographs are remarkable in a number of ways: many are beautifully composed, some are dramatic, many are evocative. Did the photographer recognise the quality of the images? Few of the photographs contain people; they were, after all, a record of the buildings - not of their inhabitants.

'Backyard Brighton' was the most popular of the four books originally published jointly by the Lewis Cohen Urban Studies Centre at Brighton Polytechnic and QueenSpark Books during the 1980s and early 1990s. Two thousand copies of the first edition sold out within six weeks, another edition of 2,000 copies followed shortly afterwards, a third was published a few years later. Backyard Brighton has been out of print for several years, yet we are continually being asked for copies.

This present edition of 'Backyard Brighton' has been completely re-edited, it includes new background information, further interviews, quotations from official reports and newspaper articles, newly discovered photographs and a 1930s street map. This edition has been published by Brighton Books Publishing which has inherited the publishing venture of the Lewis Cohen Urban Studies Centre at the University of Brighton.

Selma Montford

opposite: rear of 30 Richmond Hill 1935

Introduction

The poorer medieval inhabitants of Brighton lived mainly on the beach, beneath the cliffs. When encroachment by the sea made this impossible the working town transferred to the cliff top and squeezed itself roughly into the area bounded by East, North and West Streets. By the time of the French attack in 1514 this process was nearly complete. This move did not change their way of life; even a century later there were still four times as many fishermen in the town as landsmen.

With the advent of the gentry after 1750 elegant houses started to be built around the edge of the Steine. The influx of wealth drew to the town a large number of poor people to service the wealthy incomers, and at the same time many of the local fishermen were being displaced from the old town as it steadily gentrified. Between 1790 and 1820 the population grew from around 3,000 to 30,000. As a consequence humble housing for this tidal wave of population was built around the fringes of the town, up the hill to the east of the Steine and along the slope to the west of the Old Town, approximately the areas we call Carlton Hill and Churchill Square today.

At the foot of the down rising above the Steine on the east ran the bridleway to Rottingdean. To the south of this track, on the level land on the top of the low cliffs, development for the wealthy had grown since 1770. To the north of the track the empty down known as Hilly Laine, was divided into five 'furlongs' by tracks called leakways. The roads that we know today follow the leakways, and Edward Street is the old bridleway itself. Carlton Hill is the division between the first and second furlongs, Sussex Street between the second and third, Richmond Hill between the third and fourth and Albion Hill between the fourth and fifth.

The furlongs were again divided into the long and narrow strips typical of medieval agriculture - strips as long as five hundred yards and as little as twelve feet wide, known a 'paul pieces'. There were over 7000 paul pieces, all oriented north-south. This ownership pattern is indelibly imprinted in the layout of the streets that grew up on them, and which we still see today.

How were these areas developed?

The growth of the area covered in this book started around 1810 largely in the section between Edward Street and Carlton Hill, in the First or Home Furlong. By 1820 this section up to Egremont Place had been developed and the Second Furlong, between Carlton Hill and Sussex Street, was begun. By 1830 the Third Furlong was started, between Sussex Street and Albion Hill. After 1830 there was a pause until around 1860 when the railway produced another surge of development.

opposite: rear of William Street showing the small adjoining back yards 1936

When the grander houses facing the Steine had been built, the land behind them was used for all the small industrial and commercial needs of the town, such as lime kilns, horse stables, warehousing, forges and piggeries; but the pressure for housing soon led to change. A developer would have to assemble four or more paul pieces to get sufficient width of land to enable both sides of a street to be laid out. Failing that he might lay out one side of a street, hoping at some time that someone would build on the other side. If a paul piece was left between developments he (or she, for women were also active in the land market at the time) would fit a single row of cottages between the larger streets. Thus came our long, narrow, north-south streets, and the one-sided streets of the narrow alleys inserted between the larger streets.

Although there were thousands of the paul pieces they were owned by less than two dozen large proprietors, but their holdings were scattered. Complications arose from the fact that the ownership of the land was based upon ancient and curious manorial practices. The paul pieces were often sold on several times and the eventual developer was in general a small local builder. He would often lay out a plan for the land, erect one or two houses, sell them to pay the mortgage and then sell the remaining land for others to continue the street. The eventual landlords, especially by the early twentieth century - the period covered by this book - were usually people of very modest means living not far away. A typical cottage could be erected for £40, and the rent it could command was £4 per annum.

Why build so meanly?

The houses were erected speculatively and built of the cheapest materials readily to hand, usually bungaroosh, before the days of damp courses. Bungaroosh is a mixture of lime mortar, beach sand, beach pebbles, clunch chalk and brickbats that is peculiar to much of central Brighton. From its salt content bungaroosh has the unhappy knack of absorbing water, so walls stream with water if unheated. It serves quite well, even without a damp course, if well maintained and heated, but the level of rents that these small buildings could command from the poor tenants did not allow for any maintenance. Needless to say with land the price it was in Brighton the houses were crowded cheek by jowl, often with further houses squeezed between or behind the original ones, in the form of courts facing inwards, behind the houses facing the street. An additional pressure to build small was that houses rated at less than £10 per annum did not attract the levy of a Poor Rate on the landlord.

These dwellings were erected before the great mid-Victorian enlightenment that sewage and health were inextricably mixed. Cholera was the ever-present shadow at the feast of early Victorian expansionism. They were also built before Thomas Crapper produced the water closet. So these buildings had outside shared privies draining only into the chalk soil. Even cesspits were rare, and at best ash pits were used. Ironically, whilst the houses were usually unlocked the privies were secured, with each

opposite: a typical Brighton backyard in the mid 1930s

OKADE OKADE

householder having a key. Water for the houses was drawn mostly from nearby wells, with inevitable consequences.

To spread the burden of finding the rent each week, lodgers were usually taken in so that overcrowding became endemic. In one case 19 people were found to be living in a house which could scarcely accommodate a family of four. Close proximity also meant vermin, and it was not unusual for the house to scrape together two or three shillings - a week's rent - to have a building fumigated. Sadly the bugs then promptly moved back in from adjoining houses. The cry of the harassed housewife was, "They're not our bugs but next door's".

Poor but Proud

Brighton avoided the worst deprivation of the industrial cities because there was always some food in the form of free fish scraps available from the beach or the many smokeries, known as 'herring dees'. Lack of money was a constant, and the pawnshop and the fearsome Board of Guardians were a necessary resort to get through each week, but the workhouse was defied. The battle against dirt was unremitting. The weekly washday and the bathing in tin baths were important memories of family life.

Women were so closely tied to the house that they rarely left it, even sending children out to do the shopping. When the man of the house was in work the food was substantial. The people who lived there speak warmly of the community and the pleasures of life, of the Good Friday skipping (still maintained in Alciston) and the 'Maying' by youngsters dressed in paper. Children of the time have happy memories. Schools provided material help as well as instruction. Holidays and Sunday School outings were savoured. Close observers of the time remark that there was little real criminality, despite drunkenness amongst the men. Some vendettas amongst the Italian ice-cream fraternity and the French onion sellers occasionally erupted, but in general these foreign groups lived easily in the community.

The Solution of the Thirties

The problem faced in Brighton was one of small houses crowded close together, with inadequate sanitation, poor water supply and overcrowding. However to many of the inhabitants they were cosy neighbourhoods with strong social support networks.

Enter the Medical Officer of Health, condemning areas wholesale. Behind him came Council officers, showing singular lack of consideration for the inhabitants and adopting a lofty 'we know best' approach. The documents of the time offend us by their officiousness: the level of compensation was niggardly, Compulsory Purchase Orders are blunt instruments and caused distress. Under the 1925 Act compensation was paid out at a figure set by the Council that considered only the value of the land, the value of the buildings, businesses and goodwill were ignored. At times the Council

opposite: backyard - with hip bath - of Regent Court at 12 Regent Hill mid 1930s

appears to have been dealing dishonestly by buying cheap and selling dear - see the section on Hayllar's Cottages.

The Council in the 1930s behaved slightly better than the Town Commissioners in 1844. Wanting to demolish two areas roughly on the site of the present Clock Tower in order to drive through a new thoroughfare from the station, they invited the inhabitants of Durham and Petty France to a free party on The Level. Whilst the residents were enjoying themselves men moved in and demolished their homes. The comments of the inhabitants are not recorded.

The consequence of the wholesale destruction in the 1930s were the outlying estates of Moulsecoomb and Whitehawk. One resident who was moved said many like her were completely disoriented. 'It was a far cry from the city life in the backstreets, with Gran up the road and Mum across the way'. Many still speak today of their unhappiness at being moved. Council officers failed to consider the close street life, extended families and social support networks of the old areas.

Why So Slow to Act?

Why was this overcrowded housing allowed to continue for so long, and why was there the sudden flurry of activity in the 1930s? The answer is money - money to buy the houses at full market value, money to demolish them, money to rehouse people. Private landlords could see no sense in making improvements since to pipe in water would turn a two shilling tenement into a three shilling one and that meant the inhabitants either went hungry or decamped owing rent.

In the first two decades of the 20th century, the emphasis moved to the provision of alternative housing, but these houses were promptly filled by those who could afford them. This was the era of Patcham, Ovingdean and Woodingdean. Houses described in Backyard Brighton remained untouched. As recently as 1939 the Brighton, Hove & Preston Blanket Lending Society still lent blankets out to families for the winter for just a shilling.

It was not until the Greenwood Act of 1930, which offered considerable subsidies to tackle the slums by demolition, that actions were taken. When funds became available Local Authorities fell over themselves to produce plans for clearance. Brighton was no exception. The destruction continued from the mid 30s until the Second World War put a stop to it, but continued after the War, in the '50s and the '60s.

The town was not unique in photographing the condemned houses before demolition though the quality of many of the Brighton photographs is outstanding.

Derek Burns

opposite: rear of Richmond Hill, between Carlton Hill and Sussex Street, mid 1930s

Preface

In the following interviews those who actually lived in these old streets and courts speak for themselves about what life was really like in Backyard Brighton. They are richly evocative of a way of life it is hard for us nowadays to comprehend. Views might differ amongst them of the real merits of life in their small houses but one thing shines through - a sense of life and liveliness that pulsed vigorously through these narrow streets.

The roads are listed roughly in the sequence that they were built, running from the first decade of the nineteenth century through to the 1860s. Each street has a short preamble to explain where it was located.

The residents of Backyard Brighton used 'old money' - when they had any. To understand the very tiny sums that constituted the whole budgets of poor people in the 1930s and 1940s they can be converted roughly as follows. All the terms noted appear in the interviews. The speakers also use slang and semi slang terms for coins, and these are included.

halfpenny / ha'porth / half penn'orth	0.2 new pence
one penny / penn'orth	0.4 new pence
tuppence / two penn'orth	0.8 new pence
thruppence	1.2 new pence
sixpence / tanner	2.5 new pence
shilling / bob	5 new pence
one pound (weight)	half a kilogram (roughly)

Converting the sums does not give us any idea of their actual value at the time. Some clues are contained in the costs of common foodstuffs quoted by interviewees, but as a guide it might help to note that an average working man's wage in these decades was £1.50 to £2 per week in the early years, rising to £4 per week at the end of the two decades. Today the average wage of the bottom 50% of the population is around £460 per week, some 230 times as much as in the Thirties, which would make one old penny worth about a pound in today's money, and an old shilling about twelve pounds.

Such conversions are only a guide.

opposite: Marine View, between Carlton Hill and Park Road Terrace 1935. The houses faced the wall of the Zylo works. The firm had bought the houses because of complaints about noise.

overleaf: map of central Brighton 1882

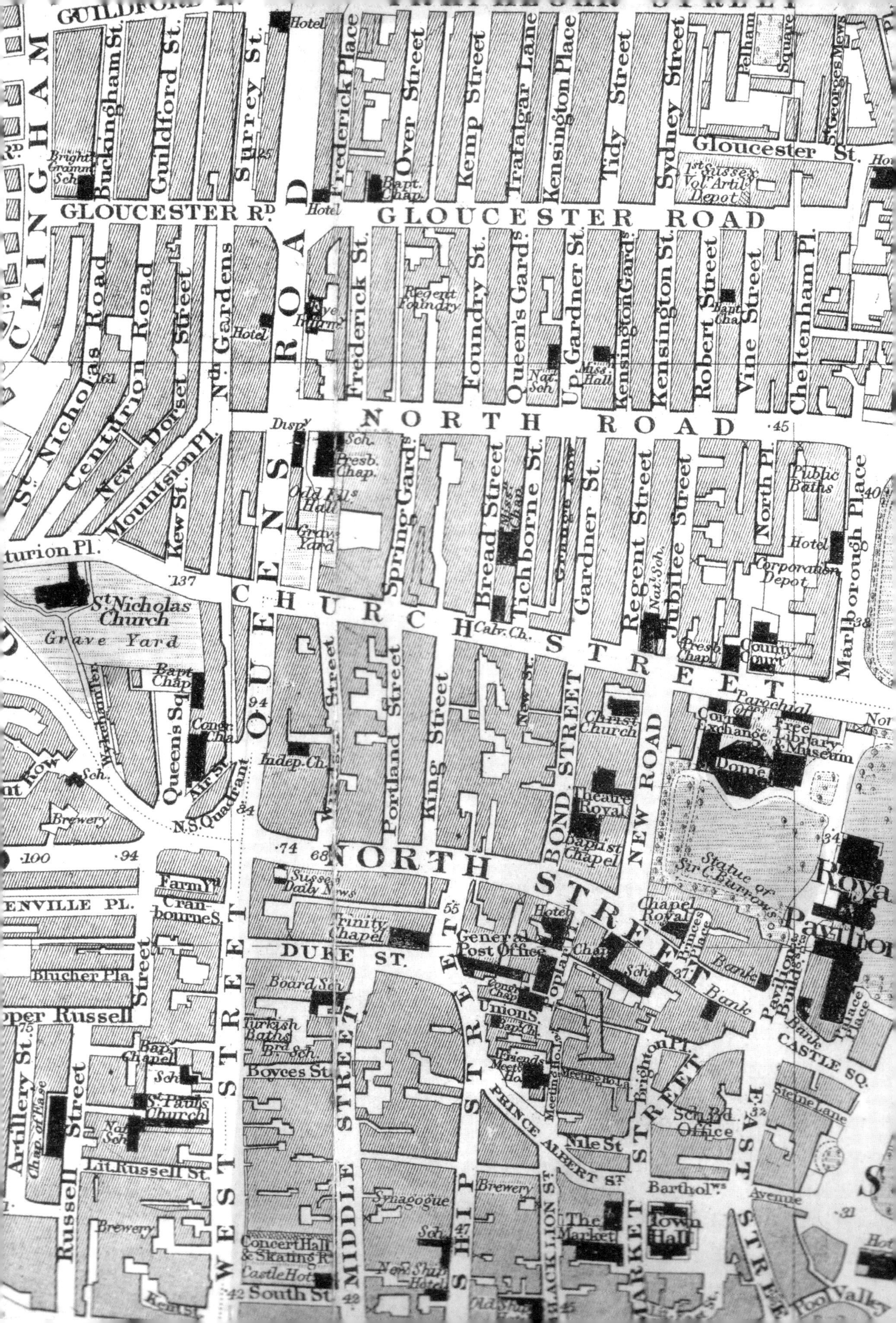

GLOUCESTER ROAD
GLOUCESTER Rd.
Buckingham St.
Guildford St.
Surrey St.
Frederick Place
Over Street
Kemp Street
Trafalgar Lane
Kensington Place
Tidy Street
Sydney Street
Pelham Square
St. Georges Mews
Gloucester St.
1st Sussex Vol. Artil. Depot
Bapt. Chap.
Hotel
St. Nicholas Road
Centurion Road
New Dorset Street
Nth Gardens
Frederick St.
Regent Foundry
Foundry St.
Queen's Gards.
Up. Gardner St.
Kensington Gards.
Kensington St.
Robert Street
Vine Street
Cheltenham Pl.
Nat. Sch.
Miss. Hall
NORTH ROAD
Mountsion Pl.
Kew St.
Sch.
Presb. Chap.
Odd Fllws Hall
Grave Yard
Spring Gards.
Bread Street
Tichborne St.
Gardner St.
Regent Street
Jubilee Street
North Pl.
Public Baths
Marlborough Place
Corporation Depot
Centurion Pl.
St. Nicholas Church
Grave Yard
CHURCH STREET
QUEENS ROAD
Calv. Ch.
Presb. Chapl.
County Court
Parochial Offices
Free Library & Museum
Corn Exchange
Dome
Bapt. Chap.
Queen's Sq.
Congr. Cha.
Air St.
N.S. Quadrant
Wykeham Ter.
Brewery
Indep. Ch.
Portland Street
King Street
New St.
BOND STREET
NEW ROAD
Christ Church
Theatre Royal
Baptist Chapel
Statue of Sir C. Burrows
NORTH STREET
Royal Pavilion
Farm Yd.
Cranbourne S.
Sussex Daily News
Trinity Chapel
Chapel Royal
Princes Place
DUKE ST.
General Post Office
Bank
Blucher Pla.
Upper Russell
Board Sch.
Union S.
Bap. Ch.
Friends Meeting Ho.
Meeting Ho. La.
Brighton Pl.
Pavilion Buildgs.
Palace Place
CASTLE SQ.
Turkish Baths
Brd. Sch.
Boyces St.
Bap. Chapel
Sch.
St. Pauls Church
Nat. Sch.
Artillery St.
Chap. of Ease
Russell Street
Lit. Russell St.
WEST STREET
MIDDLE STREET
SHIP STREET
PRINCE ALBERT ST.
Nile St
MARKET STREET
EAST STREET
Sch. Bd. Office
Steine Lane
Bartholws. Avenue
Brewery
Synagogue
BLACK LION ST.
The Market
Town Hall
Concert Hall & Skating Rk.
Castle Hotel
New Ship Hotel
South St.
Pool Valley

RICHMOND STREET
HILL
Richmond
Ashton
Dinapore
Liverpool
Chap.
Board Sch. Girls
Sussex P.
Ivory Pl.
Claremont Row
Claremont St.
Claremont Pl.
Board Sch. Boys
GRAND PARADE
Cong. Cha.
SUSSEX STREET
Meth. Cha.
Bapt. Chap.
Windmill Street
Stanley St.
Circus Street
Carlton Row
Woburn Place
Nelson Row
Nelson Place
Nelson Street
Carlton Street
Richmond Hill
Nat. Sch.
Board Sch.
Tilbury P.
St. John's Church
Lennox St.
Marine V.
Carlton P.
U. Park P.
Lodge
Egremont Gate
Park Hill
CARLTON HILL
Brighton & Sussex Sch. of Art
Cath. Ap. Chap.
William Street
Henry Street
John Street
Mighell Street
Cumberland P.
Thomas Street
Nat. Sch.
Chesterfield St.
Derby Place
Grovenor St.
Devonshire St.
Mt. Pleasant
Industr. Home
Egremont Place
Almsh.
Leicester St.
Spa Street
Egremont Street
Park St.
Riding Sch.
EDWARD STREET
Pav. S.
Princes St.
Steine Gd.
Dorset St.
George St.
Dorset Gards
2
Cavendish St.
HIGH STREET
Lecture Room
Chapel Street
Devonshire Pl.
Upr. Rock Gards
Nat. Sch.
Mount Street
Lavender St.
Meth. Cha.
Sch.
St. James's Cha.
St. Mary's Cha.
Brewery
ST. JAMES'S STREET
Miss. Hall
Steine St.
Manchester St.
Charles St.
Broad St.
German Pl.
Camelford S.
Margaret S.
Wentworth S.
NEW STEINE
Rock Pl.
Lower Rock Gardens
Atlingworth S.
Police Sta.
UP. S
GRAFTON ST.
Wyndham St.
MARINE
Grand Aquarium

United
ALES
THE THREE
KINGS.
AND

Cavendish Street

Cavendish Street is one of only two streets in this book that lie to the south of Edward Street. It was the earliest to be built, before 1808, but at that time was called Cumberland Street. It did not become Cavendish Street until 1820. There is still a street of that name, at the top end of St James's Street, but it is now just a brief stub end in amongst a jumble of industrial and high rise Council buildings.

Margaret Hamon tells us about life in Cavendish Street:

We were born at 48 Cavendish Street after my mother had done a 'moonlight flit' from Woburn Place to Cavendish Street because the rent was cheaper at 3 shillings a week. She was expecting me when she was widowed at the age of 46 and needed a cheaper house to live in. When she viewed the house in daylight she didn't see the rats, as it had all been done up.

My father had brought home a bayonet from World War One as a souvenir and my mother used it to chop the rats in half as they came down the chimney. She became furious after my sister had walked down the stairs with a rat clinging to her upper lip. She went to the Health Department to complain and spoke to a pompous man who said, 'Mrs Hamon, they're probably mice, you probably wouldn't know what a rat looked like'.

So, she killed a rat, wrapped it up in newspaper and she threw it at the man and said 'Now tell me I don't know what rats are'. 'The Evening Argus' got hold of the story because my sister had to go to the Sussex County and be treated. Instead of moving us from Cavendish Street, which was the worst slum in modern history, they moved us across the road to number 20. We didn't get rats inside that house but my oldest brother used to have to stand with a candle in a jam jar while we went to the toilet in the back yard because we were terrified of them out there.

My mother had eleven children but three had died in infancy, and she also took in her dead sister's three children to prevent them going into the Workhouse. When my father died my mother went down Edward Street to the Board of Guardians and asked them for help. She told them the plight she was in, trying to raise her sister's children and her own, so they came up to look at the house. They said 'You can put four children in that bed and four children in that bed and sell that spare bed. You can sell those chairs and let the children sit on the floor or on the bench to eat'. So they gave her nothing.

My father had been a hawker and had a stable in Jubilee Street. He had suffered gas poisoning in The Great War and had shrapnel in his head that they said was too near the brain to operate on. He used to get tremendous headaches and was always retching into a bucket. One day he collapsed in the stable and his horse stomped on

opposite: The Three Kings public house at 26 Edward Street 1930s

him and he died. The horse and cart were sold and a friend of my father's got my mother a barrow and the first vegetables to sell. She pushed this barrow around the streets selling vegetables in all weathers to earn the money to keep her family. Standing out in all weathers ruined her health and she had bad rheumatic fever in later life.

Cavendish Street was a busy little street with a pie shop, a pub, coal merchants, bakers, grocers, general shops, antique dealers, electrical suppliers, boot repairers, hairdressers and the St James Hall. At the bottom of it there was Nyer's Yard. If they had a show at the Hippodrome the animals, like the elephants, were kept there.

Edward Street before road widening between 1961-4. The Thurlow Arms, on the left, is on the corner of George Street. W A Hooker, baker, is on the right on the corner of John Street

There were quite a few Italian families living in the street (the Marcantonios, Demascios and Varrellas). They didn't like their daughters going out with the local boys. My mother's brother married a girl from an Italian family and he had a very happy marriage, but her family never learnt to speak English.

Cavendish Street houses had gas mantles for light and a range for cooking. They were warm downstairs but extremely cold upstairs. We used to buy coal from Riding School Lane where there was a woman who sold it. She was as thin as a rasher of wind but she used to shovel the coal in with a huge shovel while you held the bag open. She'd then lift up the sack and weigh it and you'd push it home on a pram. One day when she was talking I tried to lift the shovel but I couldn't. How that woman picked up that shovel I'll never know.

When my mother was short of fuel she'd make parcels from vegetable peelings to bank the fire up. If you walked through the house you'd think she was cooking us a lovely dinner.

Once she said to my sister and I, 'There's road works at the bottom of Carlton Hill, but look out for the watchman'. He'd have this little brazier to keep him warm and he was there to stop people taking the blocks of wood that had been dug up from the roadway. What came out had to be fitted in again.

We sneaked up with this old pram but the watchman got hold of me and shook me like a bundle of wet rags. And what did my sister do? She went off home with the wood. But when we put it on the fire it went 'ping, ping, ping' - the black tar on them went pinging round the room and we were forever ducking.

When the rent man came around wearing his satchel we would have to be quiet if my mother didn't have the money. We would sit inside the house and laugh. He would call out 'I know you're in there. I can hear you breathing' and she would call back 'I've got no money. I'm feeding my children', and he would go away.

My mum would take us shopping down St James's Street to the 'Home & Colonial' stores. In the window there used to be a big bowl of cheap, cracked eggs.

My sister and I were often sent to a butcher's shop opposite Woolworths where we had to ask for half a pound of cooked udder. We wouldn't say the word udder so my mum would have to give us a note. Every time we went in the butcher would look at the note and shout it out and we would go red. We had to eat that udder for our dinner in between bread and you could have soled shoes with it.

Years ago if people didn't have enough food they would borrow things like an onion or potatoes. And one of them would make a big stew and share it with the neighbours.

I went to St John the Baptist School when I was three. If you said to the nuns, 'Sister, we haven't had any breakfast' we could go down where the kitchens were and they would give you a cup of cocoa and a piece of bread and dripping. The nuns were very fair. If children brought sweets to school they would put them in a jar and open it on Friday and give them to all the children. The Headmistress was kind but could be strict. She used to say 'Come here, you heathens', and she called my sister 'The child of the devil'.

During the war we were transferred to St John's in Carlton Hill because it was nearer our home, but I didn't like it as I thought they were spiteful. There wasn't bullying like today but there was name-calling. One reason was that my mother was allowed to get free shoes for the children on a voucher from Laceys in Trafalgar Street. They were always black, but on the side of the shoe would be a 'C' for Corporation to stop people pawning them. My sisters tried to scrape the 'C' off the shoes because the other kids would kick your shoes and say 'Oh look, she's got Corporation shoes'.

In the War there was a shop on the corner of William Street and Carlton Hill (photo page 84) and it was something to do with the Germans. Rumour had it that the woman owner hid her sons so that they wouldn't be interned during the war.

The pub at the top of George Street Gardens and Carlton Hill was called 'The Italian Arms' and they made them change the name to 'The Carlton Arms' because we were at war with the Italians and people didn't like it.

In September 1939 we were moved to the St John's Place. They were brand new houses, even the front door hadn't been screwed on. When we went there we stood with our mouths open because everything looked so clean and bright, and there was a bathroom and a toilet inside the house.

You could have a copper for an additional three shillings a week, and an electric fire for a bit more. There was also a plug-in iron that my mother thought was marvellous because she'd only ever had a flat iron before. My mother was absolutely delighted.

Everyone was poor in Cavendish Street, but when you lived in a street you felt that you weren't isolated, you were all one family.

William Street

William Street 1936

William Street still exists, it runs north from the bottom of Edward Street to Carlton Hill.

Georgina Attrell grew up in William Street, a wide street of substantial three or four storey houses with bow windows, different from many of the surrounding cramped cottages. It was originally called North Steyne Row. The houses had small gardens that opened on to Sun Street, but that did not save them from demolition, as they lacked basic amenities. Later interviews suggest that the street had gained a bad reputation by the early twentieth century, perhaps because there were a number of lodging houses.

Georgina Attrell remembers:

Some people have described William Street as a 'slum', but I remember it quite differently. I recall the houses as being quite large by today's standards. Most of them had basements with several storeys above. The occupants were all working-class - fishermen, labourers, general dealers, with a baker at number 29. Five houses were lodging houses. Fishing was the dominant occupation. Those men lived life with all the dangers and even death that fishing from open boats can bring.

Carlton Hill was a haven for foreign refugees and immigrants. The 'hokey pokey' trade (ice cream) was very common. I watched for hours while 'Pip' Pirolli made and mixed his product.

Ours was a small, single room, lit by an oil lamp, with an open grate that burned both winter and summer. The room boasted only the barest of essentials: a double bed, a

LIFEBUOY
FOR HEALTH SOAP
OLISH
for
FLOORS FURNITURE, LINO ETC
COLMAN'S
STARCH
29 S.A.GOLDRING. 29
HUDSON'S
HUDSON'S

table, some kitchen chairs and an old-fashioned, heavy chest of drawers. There was a small mat in front of the fire and the rest of the floor was covered with what we called 'oil cloth', the forerunner of linoleum.

We had the use of the wash house or scullery once a week to do the washing. The 'privy' was a little brick shed at the end of the yard, with a wooden seat and a step which was always scrubbed white. It was simple, but it was home and I loved it.

Wash day was a mammoth affair, always on a Monday, come rain or shine. Mum and Gran got up at dawn to light the brick built copper with the galvanised pan. They kept it stoked with the rubbish from a local sweet shop. They wore aprons made from empty sugar sacks scrounged from the grocer at the end of the street. Two wooden tubs were hauled into the yard and filled with boiling water softened with soda crystals. With the wash board and a stiff brush, battle commenced.

The 'whites' were put into the copper and boiled, with a twopenny packet of Hudson's washing powder and a bar of Sunlight soap. The other clothes were scrubbed in the tubs. The place was like a steam bath. The tubs were then emptied; one was filled with clear water, the other with blue water. This was made with a penny Reckitts Blue (a blue block of powder tied in a little muslin bag), swished about in the tub. It made the rinse that gave the clothes that 'whiter than white' look that we hear so much about these days. Starch came in chalky lumps, which was mixed smooth with boiling water and then cold water added. It produced a bluey-grey, glue-like substance that stiffened everything from Dad's collars to the pillow cases.

Both Mum and Gran took it in turns at the handle of the great mangle with wooden rollers. Then it was all out on the line to dry. They took pride in the wash, and got great pleasure in seeing the clothes pegged out on the line.

Times were good when Dad worked, and we fed like kings - meat puddings and pies, stews, new bread, bacon puddings and bread pudding. We had no stove, so cooking was done on the open fire. Everything that needed to be baked had to be taken down to the bakers at the corner of Steine Gardens. For a penny he would cook it in his bread ovens and we collected it when we came from school.

Down at the Fish Market early in the morning you could watch the catches of herring and mackerel being sold off. Fish was very cheap and formed the staple diet of many of us as children. When times were hard Mum made a dinner from conger eel and parsley sauce. I hated it, but it was better than being hungry. In Carlton Row there were the herring dees, where they smoked herrings caught locally. They were strung in pairs on long poles over the smoke from fires. We were often sent for two penn'orth of remnants. Breakfasts were bread and margarine in the summer, and toast with margarine - or if we were lucky with dripping - made on the kitchen range for winter.

opposite: William Street 1930s, built between 1809-1821. The arched entrance was Lou Morris's boarding house. The shop in the top picture was S A Goldring, baker

We only had fresh milk on Sunday, when George James came round with the churn. Fish and chips was a real treat. There was a lovely fish and chip shop in Edward Street where you could buy a bag of 'scraps' for half a penny. Lillywhite's the fruit shop, on the corner of Steine Gardens, sold 'two penn'orth of specks', fruit that was bruised or soft. At Giggin's the bakers, in Grand Parade, we got our clean pillowcase filled with stale bread for fourpence each morning before we went to school.

The grocer's shop that I remember best was Corder's, on the corner of William Street and Carlton Hill. This was like an Aladdin's Cave. You took your bottle to buy the vinegar, and a jam jar for jam. Everything was loose and had to be weighed and put into thick blue paper bags. Sugar, rice, soda and all the dried fruit came in Hessian sacks. We bought soap in a long bar, about ten or twelve inches long, and what you required was cut off. Soap was always bought long before you needed it and stored so that it went hard; that way it lasted longer.

My brother George and I would take Dad's dinner down to him at midday. It would be wrapped in a cloth, and steaming hot in a basket, together with a jug of tea. Poor Dad worked as a building labourer and his hands were always chapped and raw, so he carried something called a Melrose Tablet in his pocket. It looked like a ball of yellow grease and he used it to lubricate his hands.

Mum knitted a lot, and sometimes spent all night sitting by candle-light knitting so that she could earn a few shillings making jumpers. She used to knit fishermen's jerseys too, and as they took longer she got more money for them. She also sewed, and made me clothes when she could afford it.

They were lovely times with Dad in work. We used to go for bus rides along the front and to Rottingdean. There was a little single decker bus like a charabanc that used to run from the top of Elm Grove to the Downs Hotel and walked down to Rottingdean and then got a bus home along the front. In summer my Mum would take all of us kids down to the beach for the day. We had bread and marge for dinner, and lemonade made up from yellow powder bought from a little shop at the bottom of William Street. We'd watch the boats taking the trippers out to sea and we would help the fishermen pull the boats up on to the beach between each trip. If we were lucky old Mr Rolf would take us out for a ride.

This happy situation was not long-lived, for the start of the thirties brought unemployment and hunger. I used to go with my Dad sometimes to wait in the long queue in Steine Gardens at the bottom of Edward Street for the dreaded Parish Relief. We were always hungry, or so it seemed. Looking back it must have been a nightmare for Mum and Dad. School time was always welcome, as we were warm there. The teachers understood our plight and would encourage us to run and exercise in the small playground. I hated being poor, and even now I can remember the times when we had holes in our shoes. During prayer times in the hall we had to kneel on the floor and I was always conscious of the state of the soles of my shoes. I never blamed my Dad. How could I? I loved him. After all, most of the kids were in the same boat.

Conditions could be bad, proper diets were non-existent. A lot of children died young. Rickets was a prevalent disease, when little legs became like broomsticks and were often crooked. Consumption, or TB as we know it now, was a dreaded word. With the damp houses and bug infested bedrooms children grew up with the smell of dankness and illness. Not many people saw the doctor as that cost money. If he came to you it cost half a crown, but you could get a ticket to the Dispensary in Ditchling Road and the doctor there would make you up something for a shilling. As money was so tight people had to be really bad before they went to the doctor.

When times were very hard there was always 'Uncle', the pawnshop in Edward Street, which had a never-ending queue of people on a Monday morning. The little office where we took the things to raise the money to feed us all for the week was a dark, gloomy little room with a very high counter. You passed the items over the counter - Dad's best suit and shoes usually, with any spare sheets and blankets that could be spared in the warmer weather and occasionally some of Gran's jewellery. If the things were clothes these would be wrapped in bits of cloth and secured with a special pin, which we knew as 'pawnshop pins'.

On Fridays we would get the items out; unredeemed pledges were of course sold off. Many's the time I've seen something that belonged to us for sale in the window of the shop in Edward Street. I hated the place and was ashamed to be seen going in. If there was anyone else there that I knew I would walk around until they had gone.

Despite this poverty, life for a child in the '20s and '30s was on the whole extremely happy. Grown-ups looked after them well, and they were protected and loved. The 'Ladies of Pleasure' in the street were always good to us, and usually gave the kids a party at Christmas. We made all our games, the greengrocer gave us the yellow rope that came around the boxes of oranges and we could throw one end over the arm of a lamppost, tie a knot and sit on it to swing. Woe betide you if the lamp lighter came round! Marbles or 'alleys', as they were called, were played in the gutter, and 'buttons' were played on the pavement. You drew a box with chalk up against the wall, and then wrote OXO on it. On the edge of the kerb you drew a ring for the start and then shot buttons in the box with your thumb and forefinger.

The Fish Market was the scene of great jollity on Good Friday every year. They would have the great scaffolding ropes, nearly two inches thick, which the men would turn, one across the other to form a cross. The grown-ups and children would skip in the middle and we'd all sing 'One a penny, two a penny, hot cross buns'. It didn't matter what size the Mums were, they all had a go in the ropes. If you missed a skip and the ropes hit your legs it was painful. How I loved Good Fridays, and for weeks before we would count the days to it.

Nelson Street

Nelson Street is no more. It is now that part of John Street which runs just uphill from the Kingswood Flats, near the Police Station. Local people still call that part of the road Nelson Street. It was one of the early streets to be built, before 1810, and compared to later nearby alleys was wide and airy with many buildings fronted by cobble masonry.

Charlotte Storrey recalls that Nelson Street was very poor:

I was born in Nelson Street. My mother was born at the bottom of Carlton Hill, in a little close called Ivory Buildings. Grandfather was a fisherman, and Ivory Buildings contained many fishermen's families. My other grandfather was a costermonger who stabled his ponies in Richmond Hill. My mother had eleven or twelve children who were all born in Nelson Street. My parents also ran a shop in Sussex Street and I worked there when I left school at fourteen. I was nineteen when I married, and I went to live at Herbert Road with my husband, but I didn't like it and we returned to live with my parents, and I ran the shop.

I can remember the sanitary man visiting us. He would walk into the house without knocking - our doors were never locked - and walk straight up to the bedrooms and pull back the bedclothes to check for bugs.

I remember the pubs in the area. One [at 119 Sussex Street] on the corner of Nelson Place was called 'The Highbury Barn' and another was called 'The Lion & Unicorn' or 'The Blue House', which was a bugbear of a place. Many soldiers and sailors drank there, and there were always fights. We had a lamp post outside our window and they used to swing on it as they left the pub, and as kids we would watch the shadows of them through the window. Women had fights as well and I remember one woman, who had a fish barrow in Claremont Place, being hit with a poker by another woman. It used to be called 'murder alley' up there.

We were very unhappy when we had to leave the area because of the demolition since we had a good business, being the only shop in that particular area. My mother died before we were moved, but we took my father and younger brother with us to Pankhurst Road, where we lived for the next 40 years. The sad thing was that our old homes stood empty for fourteen or fifteen years before they were demolished so we needn't have moved.

From the Borough Health Committee minutes:

Nelson Street: This is a congested area, and the houses are variously characterised by low-pitched, unhealthy basements and small well-like yards. Many of the houses are old and becoming derelict and from time to time boulder walls have to be replaced by brickwork. The owner of numbers 32 & 33 Nelson Street is prepared to sell for £250, plus surveyor's fees of 11 pounds 4 shillings and proper legal costs.

Carlton Row

Carlton Row 1935, built between 1800 -1808

Carlton Row was at the bottom of the hill, on the flat land behind Circus Street before it rises to the Milner and Kingswood Flats, and was another early development. It is now under the Municipal Market, which itself is now due to be demolished and redeveloped. It was one of the streets built on just two paul pieces, and so was narrow and confined.

Three of the residents, Rose, Winnie and Edie speak about their life there:

Carlton Row looked lovely and they were nice people who lived there. Up at the top of the street there was the muffin man who came round with a tray on his head. And one called Shylock who used to sling oranges at us which we nicked. The winkle lady used to call on Sundays. The fish sellers brought up fresh fish from the Market. But the Council stopped all the street trading and the barrow boys got pinched because you had to have a license. That was all wrong because everyone has to make a living.

In St James' Street there was Liptons, Home & Colonial, Maypole, World Stores, and Chapman's the butchers where we'd put sixpence a week on the card for Christmas. We also used to go up the pubs on Mondays to pay our Tontine [an annuity shared by subscribers to loan], a halfpenny or a penny a week. That way we got thirty shillings to spend at Christmas.

They called Carlton Row slums but I don't think they were slums. We were poor but we were very clean, and we weren't lousy. What gave the bad impression was that there were lots of lodging houses and you got these people walking up and down, but they never interfered with any of us. Our Mums could send us out all day and we'd come back safe. If there was any fighting people would say 'Come on duck, get out the way'. But we didn't want to get out the way, we liked to watch.

We were terrible kids really. Our house looked down into the backyards of John Street where they smoked the fish. We would stand up in our window and throw stones at the fish. We used to buy lots of pease pudding from Skinner's in Carlton Hill or Chapman's in St James Street and coming up George Street we would put a bit on our fingers and flick it onto the windows.

I was 14 when I left school and I went straight into the laundry, as did a lot of girls from our area. Most girls weren't the type to go into service because they had very close-knit families.

I used to get ten bob a week, and from that I got one shilling pocket money. I used to get a sixpenny pair of stockings from Halliday's in Richmond Buildings, but if you went to Woolworth's and got real silk ones they were sixpence each. You could buy one stocking one week and the other the following week. I'd sometimes buy a pair of French knickers for a shilling from Dorothy Norman's.

I also used to look after a baby in a pub. I worked from ten in the morning to ten at night for sixpence. My Mum used to take the sixpence and give me back tuppence, so I'd worked all day for just tuppence.

Our parents were very strict. If my young man took me out and we come home a bit late my mother used to stand outside near the bottom of Carlton Hill and shout 'Edie, you wait till you come in here, I'll kill you.' I would go to my mates in Milner Flats, but when I got up the hill to home I'd get a crack, I'd get a good hiding.

At the other end of Carlton Row we had a Mission Hall where there was bar billiards. I was up there once and my brother told my Mum I was up the street with a chap. She came out up the street and I didn't know how to look that bloke in the face the next night. Another time somebody told my Mum I was out at the Barracks with the soldiers, and when I got home my Mum and Dad hit me, but I wasn't anywhere near the Barracks.

We often went dancing at the end of the pier. I never had any soles on my shoes and I used to get bleeding splinters in my feet. Years ago we used to stand our plants out in the street when it rained and nobody would touch them. Nowadays they'd take your teeth and come back for your gums.

opposite: Carlton Row, between Sussex Street and Carlton Hill, mid 1930s

Albion Street

Albion Street 1976, built 1800-1808, demolished 1959

Albion Street was built around 1805, and was then one of two isolated runs of houses (the other being Richmond Place facing St Peter's Church which, though much altered, is still there) that were separated from the rest of the town by two hundred yards of open country. There is still an Albion Street on the site. The top end of the street used to be the better end. Now the position is reversed, with the top end being something of a desert, but near that end the restored cottages of Phoenix Place give us an idea of what we have lost.

Tom Gower tells of life in Albion Street:

I was born at 34 Albion Street in 1911 and continued to live there until I was married in 1933. My parents had earlier lived in other houses in Albion Street but had moved to number 34 because it was bigger for their eleven children. I was the youngest, and there were only four children at home most of the time I was growing up. My father drove a horse and cart for a building firm and then became the foreman of a timber yard in Edward Street.

The house had a cobbled front and three bedrooms, a sitting room and kitchen and scullery. We didn't have a bath in those days, but if you went into people's back yards you always saw a long tin bath hanging on the back wall. We also had an outside toilet in our small back yard which was quite smart for a toilet in those days. Ours had a wooden case in front of it. Further down the street they had toilets that backed onto the back wall and were side by side. The boys who lived there would play a joke and put their hands through the top of the adjoining toilet and pull the chain while you were sitting there.

I remember Albion Street as a very rough, old road, not tarmacked like today. We were at the top end of the street near Tamplin's Brewery. Tamplin's owned the houses and they had an agent who collected the rent of ten and fourpence every week. They kept their horses in the stables at the back of our house and every Saturday washed the whole of the brewery yard and all the water would pour down Albion Street into the drains. It helped to keep the road fresh and clean.

Our end of the street was much the quieter, with just houses and a small shop. It was really a sweet shop but you could also buy minor bits of groceries. We would take along a half-pound jam jar and they would weigh the jar and then add the jam from a very large container. You could also buy sausage, brawn and firewood. The other end of Albion Street was very overcrowded and the houses had mostly three storeys with back yards that weren't very nice. They also had a pub called the 'Albion Inn' and the Tamplin's bottling store. My sister worked there as did quite a few local people.

Billet's sweet factory was in the street. One of my friends worked there as a sugar boiler. They made all types of sweets but only had one shop, in Richmond Place, that almost backed onto their factory. We used to go into the shop and get 'a penn'orth of broken'. There were also several stables and builders who had workshops.

I went to Richmond Street School, which was one of the first schools in Brighton to be built after the 1870 Education Act. When I was there it still had gas lighting - a three-armed thing with bat-winged burners and no mantle, just had a flame. We had to light it with one boy having a taper ready on a stick and another boy with a rod to turn the gas on. Later we had mantles. Our classroom was very large with three double windows, so it could get cold. At first we had a coal fire at the front, but I was there when they fitted large radiators in the room and it was much warmer. There was a bell rope in the corner.

We stayed in the classroom for all our lessons except physical exercise and woodwork. We had football at Preston Park every Thursday afternoon and were taken to St Luke's Baths for swimming. There was no actual school uniform but we all wore ties with a claret and blue stripe, and short trousers until we left school at fourteen. The school was very strict and you would get the cane or the strap if you misbehaved.

Some of the boys in my class came from poorer families. It seemed that the nearer you lived to the sea the poorer the area got. Streets like John Street and William Street used to be rough. The houses in William Street were originally for 'gentlemen's ladies' and some of houses had probably looked quite nice when they were built, but if anyone spoke of slums the first thing you thought about was William Street. Many of the fathers were costermongers and it was quite usual to see children running about without shoes and socks in the summer. Boys weren't allowed to come to school

without shoes and socks, but boys could get Council boots - heavy hobnail boots with a wooden sole and a metal 'pout' on them that made a lot of noise and sometimes sparked on the pavement.

Claremont Row, opposite Richmond Street School, was one of the worst streets. I was friendly with a boy who lived in one of them and I went in there once. The houses were dreadful and it wouldn't have taken much for them to fall down. My home in Albion Street was a palace compared with those. The people who lived there were very poor. Carlton Row and Woburn Place were also poor and I seem to remember they had washing lines across the road.

Dorothy Betteridge also lived in Albion Street and remembers:

I lived next door to Billet's sweet factory. Opposite the house was 'The Albion' public house where they played cards, darts and shove ha'penny. They had a piano in the back room and we could hear the music coming from there in the evenings. We didn't have much trouble from the pub.

My mother was a housewife and my father was a freehand painter at the Lancing Carriage works. I had two brothers, a sister and a twin sister Gladys, or Midge as we called her. She died when she was seven from diphtheria. It was a custom on May Day to dress up in paper and go out to see people. After we had been out 'Maying' Midge complained of a sore throat. She was buried on 6th May. I then became very close to my mother and would sleep in her bed. When we heard my father's footsteps coming in from the pub I would quickly run into my own bed.

Some of my most enjoyable times were spent in the Brighton Girls' Club which was in Claremont Row. I can remember dressing in a pale blue, knitted jumper with the club badge and a short navy skirt to take part in exercises on a Sunday morning on top of the Aquarium to advertise the Club activities. We also made and sold paper flowers for the Club funds. I was conscious that Albion Street was considered to be better than Claremont Row, which my mother considered a slum. She didn't like me walking along there, but I wanted to go to the club. The houses didn't look different from ours.

When I was young I attended Richmond Street School but transferred to Circus Street after my sister Gladys died. When I was eleven I went to Pelham Street, where I did quite well with my lessons and came top of my year. I don't remember anybody sitting for the secondary school examination, and we all assumed that we would leave school at fourteen.

When I first left school I went to work for Singer's in Western Road, but I was tempted away by a shop in Over Street that offered better money. My mother made me leave there because the woman put on me to do all the housework.

opposite: the back yard of 93 Edward Street, F Cotton confectioner, c1935

Henry Street

Henry Street, between Edward Street and Carlton Hill

Henry Street is now lost under the Police Station, running through the middle of the site. The photograph is seemingly taken when demolition was already well under way, and the old houses had been taken over by light industry.

Charles Yeates worked in one of the small businesses there and recalls:

When I left school I worked at a silversmiths owned by Henry (Harry) Jacobs. It was a seven year apprenticeship starting at nine shillings a week. The firm moved to Henry Street and many people will remember H P Jacobs repairing and restoring silver there. I used to be sent to Marshall's Row to hire a barrow and load it up with silver and push it all over Brighton to return goods. I would leave the barrow unattended outside shops and never had anything taken.

Henry Street was a mixture of professions. I can remember the tall brick chimney of the kipper drying factory where the owner and his wife threaded herrings on birch rods. The smell was delicious. Opposite us was a warehouse where the onion sellers used to stay during the season. They came from Normandy in boats and brought the whole family with them. During the day the family would sit stringing onions together while the man of the family went off on his bike to sell what he could. One year, I think it was 1925, there was a terrible tragedy. After a successful season the families were travelling home by boat and a storm destroyed the boat. Everyone was drowned.

My mother had been born at a beer house called 'The Little Wonder', and she and her sister Min would dance on the counter for the customers. Her maiden name was Wink.

The one memory that sticks in my mind is the sight and sound of children's bare feet flapping on the ground - something I've not heard since.

Nelson Place

Nelson Place was one of the second generation of streets, being built in the 1820s. It is lost now under the Kingswood Flats. It was a place of good memories for Amelia Scholey who recalls:

My Dad sold watercress and took bets. The business was in my family for a hundred years. He went to the watercress beds in Surrey in a van, starting at 4.30 in the morning. He would then take the watercress that had been bunched up the night before for sale at the Market at the Town Hall. All the children helped with the cress.

On Sunday he would take a barrow of it around. You used to get a newspaper full for a penny for sandwiches for Sunday tea. It was a good living.

We didn't want to move. Ours was the only house standing in Nelson Place.

My Dad wouldn't move until they gave him a bottom flat in Milner Flats, because it had to have a yard with running water for the cress. They offered him a top floor flat first which he refused.

They smoked herrings in Nelson Place, where there were two dees, big yards where they smoked the herrings into bloaters. They used to hang them up with a stick through their heads. When the heads fell off you used to buy three penn'orth of headless bloaters. My Mum used to send us over there for two penn'orth of 'tie tails', from the ones that fell off, that's why they were tie tails. We used to have them on toast.

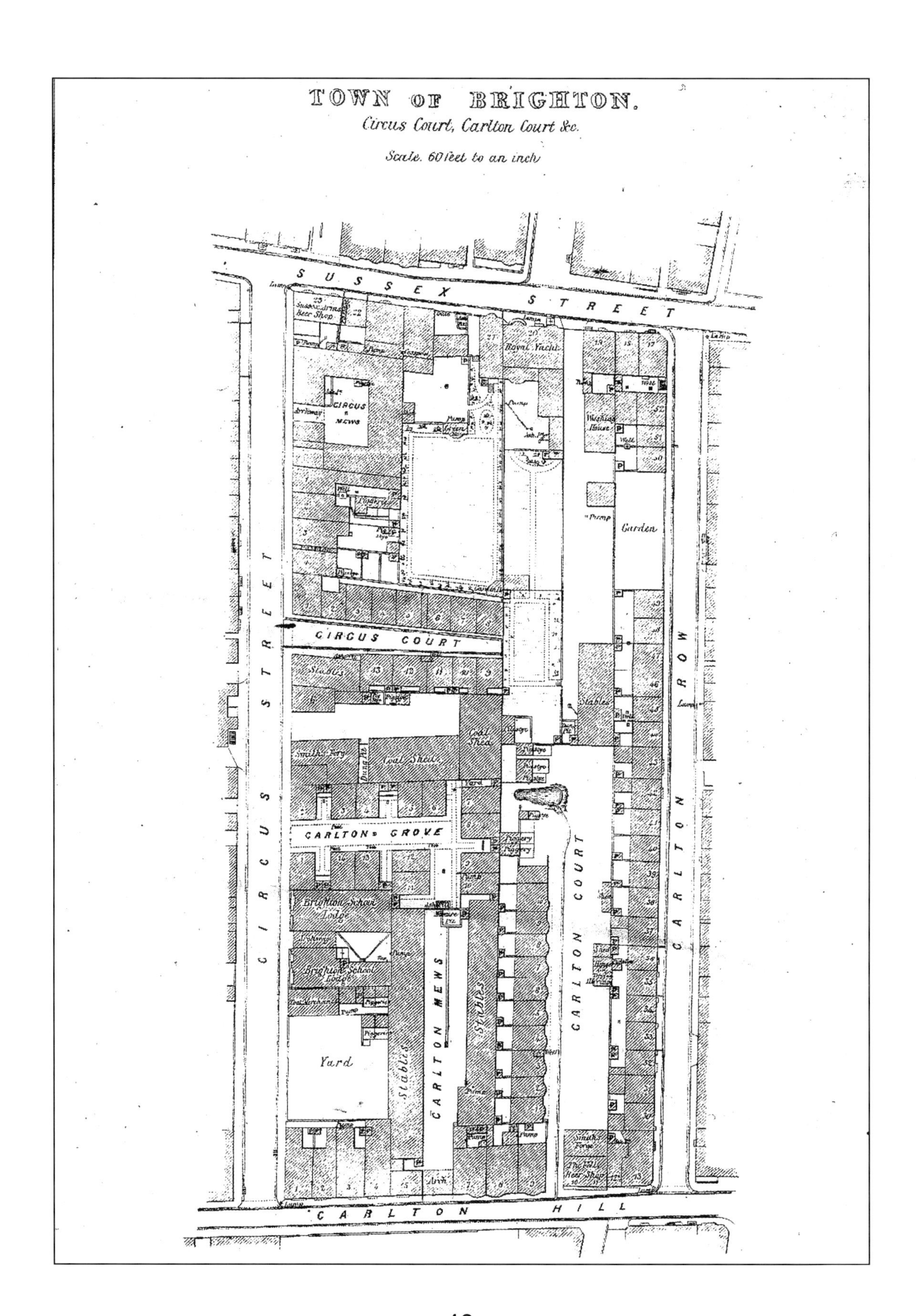
TOWN OF BRIGHTON.
Circus Court, Carlton Court &c.
Scale. 60 feet to an inch
SUSSEX STREET
CIRCUS STREET
CIRCUS COURT
CIRCUS MEWS
CARLTON GROVE
CARLTON MEWS
CARLTON COURT
CARLTON ROW
CARLTON HILL
Royal Yacht
Garden
Stables
Coal Shed
Yard
Brighton School Lodge
Smith's Forge
The Hill Beer Shop
Washing House

Circus Street

Circus Street is still exists - the home of the 24 hour Diner beloved of late night revellers and the frontage of the abandoned Municipal Market.

Circus Street runs along the back of the elegant houses on Grand Parade. It got its name from the Royal Circus and Riding School, opened in 1808 by a Mr Saunders on a site roughly where 36 Grand Parade stands today. Unfortunately the venture was not a success and it had closed by 1812, leaving only the name and that of one of the Royal residences, Carlton, to remind us of its more illustrious past.

The area quickly became a mixture of poor housing and small industrial sites, with the small gaps between the housing being used for stabling and piggeries. Archways led into the enclosed world of the Courts and Closes, where such strong community ties were formed.

The area also became a cause for concern and Health Reports published in 1840 and 1849 condemned the district. The 1849 Creasey Health Report had particular criticism of Carlton Row: 'Fever rages in this location. Several houses are mere ruins.'

Carts were unable to enter several of the Courts to remove the refuse mounds which had to be removed by hand. Nearby Carlton Grove had the sewage from fourteen cottages draining into a large cesspool situated in the middle of the courtyard, emptied only yearly, and Carlton Court contained 19 pigs in a filthy condition.

Several attempts were made to clear the more insanitary areas, but only Carlton Grove disappeared. Eventually Compulsory Purchase Orders were issued in 1931. Circus Street then still contained a mixture of housing and light industry. There was a sawdust merchant; a general stores, wholesale newsagents and a sweep and soot store as well as a school, public house and housing. Most of the businesses had traded in the area for many years and had little enthusiasm for their enforced move, especially when only minimal compensation was offered. The chimney sweep firm of Wadey's had been at number 7 Circus Street since the 1860s.

By 1937 all the buildings on the eastern side of Circus Street, except Circus Street School, had been demolished and the new Municipal Market was built. In 2005 that Market transferred to Hollingbury and the redevelopment of Circus Street is under discussion once again.

Opposite: map of part of the Carlton Hill area developed between 1800-1808, but condemned in Creasy's Health Report in 1849

Albion Cottages

Albion Cottages, rear of Albion Street, mid 1930s

Albion Cottages was an L-shaped alley that ran up the hill at right angles from Albion Street and then turned and cut through to Albion Hill. It started life as Richmond Mews around 1825. It consisted of a row of houses on one side and the blank back walls of the houses in Albion Street on the other.

W Holmes was glad to leave the alley as he recalls:

Albion Cottages had a real community spirit, stemming from the fact we were all in the same boat of being poor. For us children that meant it was obligatory that the older looked after the younger whenever we went to the beach or up to the Race Hill for the day. Parents were not over-protective then.

In the centre of the small yard at the back was a drain. Much excitement was caused one day when the old lady next door came home drunk, fell over and got her head stuck in the drain. After much struggling she was freed.

This old lady also managed to set fire to her chimney, a common occurrence in those days. As the alley was too narrow to get the fire engine in the hoses had to be run in. Since it was a washday the alley was strung with lines of fresh washing across it. It also coincided with the kids coming home from school for their dinner. The combination of sweating, swearing firemen, irate housewives trying to salvage their washing and kids skylarking and yelling, whilst over all a black pall of smoke rose, produced an absolute bedlam.

Sickness was very much a do-it-yourself affair. Sending for a doctor was unheard of because of the cost. If treatment was essential herbalists were resorted to. There was one in the Open Market, to whom my mother took me when she decided I had mumps. He produced a black ointment which was applied to me and I was cured - whether due to the ointment I would not want to say.

Children were expected to run errands in those days. I would have to go regularly to the street above ours and get a fourteen pound bag of coal. Every dinner time I had to fetch a Guinness for a neighbour from the bottom of Albion Hill. On Saturdays I would walk to Sears the grocers in Preston Road for three pennyworth of bacon pieces for a bacon pudding. Shops nearby provided everything needed for everyday living. There were two grocers, a greengrocer, a fish and chip shop, a newsagent, a barber, a shoe repairer, an undertaker, a sweep, a pub and even a cats' meat shop.

Every Sunday the Cottages were visited by the Salvation Army band, probably because my father's half brother was a band member. An annual event was the parade of decorated horses and carts from Tamplin's Brewery. The horses were decked out with ribbons, brasses and bells, and the carts were polished immaculately.

Unlike some I do not look back on those days with affection. The memories I have are of being damned cold in the winter and getting chilblains on my ears and rickets from the poor diet. Porridge was our staple diet. Rabbit was another item on the menu. I did not like it. Mother skinned the rabbits herself, and I would then have to take the skin to the rag and bone merchant nearby.

I lived in the cottages until I was ten, when our house was condemned and pulled down. The others in the alley were left and renovated and were only removed in the 1960s. The house we moved to in Manor Farm was a palace. I remember we put our few bits and pieces on the back of a lorry, climbed in and left without so much as a backward glance.

LADIES
& GENTs
HAIRDRESSING
SALOON

Carlton Street

The remains of Carlton Street could be seen on the ground until two years ago, when a block of flats was finally built on the site - half a century after the demolition of the street. The street was originally built around 1830 and stood a few yards further up the hill above the section of John Street that runs along the back of the Kingswood flats.

Several unnamed residents contributed their memories of the street and the area:

When we lived in Carlton Street we had the whole house. The sitting room was the best room. There we had a nine piece suite - all velvet, a round table, an overmantel, a mirror and a piano (bought for five bob a week). We found a harp in the cupboard and we had a gramophone, but we weren't a musical family. The chests of drawers had no paint or varnish so when we were kids we used to have to scrub them with a bucket of water and a handfull of soda. My Mum used to have lace curtains, and when she washed them she starched them. She always had nice windows. Every six months we wallpapered the passage. We cleaned the doorstep every morning. We had bugs in the house and my Mum used to paraffin the beds, but nearly all the houses had vermin.

My Mum had lino and if there was a bit of lino that wore out, the bit of wood underneath had to be scrubbed. Every year the Gypsies came by, and they used to sell those rush mats - the fair sized ones for one and six each. My Mum used to have three, one for each bedroom. We renewed them every year. We were very posh when we had new mats.

The houses were cold upstairs and we had overcoats on the beds, but it was warm downstairs because of the kitchen range. My Dad wouldn't allow us to get in debt. Everything my Mum had she had to pay for. That's why we never had anything.

Carlton Hill was supposed to be a bad area. They were supposed to be slums. We were poor but we were clean. Our homes were immaculate. You never had a lock on your door, nobody locked their doors. We pulled a leather strap through a hole in the door to lift up the latch.

Women didn't go out after they were married. My Mum used to stand indoors and say: 'Go over there and get me that bit of beef that you can see in the shop window', and we used to have to stand outside the shop and keep pointing to the bits of beef. The kids did all the shopping, because the shopkeepers took pity on the kids. My Mum never went out - but she had a very nice back yard.

opposite top: Carlton Hill mid 1930s. The King and Queen public house, which is still standing, can be seen on the left of the photograph

opposite bottom: back yard at Carlton Street, between Carlton Hill and Sussex Street

People were poor because they had big families; nearly everyone had big families, but we had a happy childhood. We would do cartwheels and acrobats all down Carlton Hill. We used to go happy jacking under the Pier (catching coins thrown from the Pier). As teenagers we used to walk along the seafront. It would be so choc-a-bloc with people.

When we had whooping cough we never had medicine. We used to have to go and stand over a tar barrel and smell it. My Mum bought tar rope, and you would have a piece of tar rope round your neck. I say it's a wonder we are all still here.

Carlton Hill was so busy. The muffin man came round on Sunday tea-time with a big tray of crumpets on his head. He made his own crumpets and he had a big bell. The milkman used to carry his urn all the way up Carlton Hill, selling milk for a penny a pint. Fish came round with the fish barrow and they also sold big lumps of ice. You could buy a big pan of sprats for a tanner. You could buy anything from a barrow.

There were shops everywhere, all around us. You didn't have to go to the town to get anything. Buskers often came round the streets. There were always people standing on corners, and tons of people on the streets. Nobody moved into the area, because nobody moved out. Neighbours used to sit on the step and talk to passers-by. This is why people didn't want to move out of the area; the community was there. They married the people who lived next door. That community feeling went when we were moved out to Whitehawk.

On the corner of nearly every street there was a pub. 'The Rising Sun' was on the corner of Sun Street, 'The John Bull' on the corner of John Street, 'The Foresters' on the corner of Henry Street, 'The Sack of Shavings' on the corner of Richmond Hill and another on the corner of Riding School Lane. Every Saturday night there were fights. We used to watch for the men to leave the pubs so that we could see the fights. They used to fight amongst themselves and they never interfered with us; the women fought too. But it was all right walking about at night.

We remember the animals being sent up Carlton Hill every week to the Slaughter House on the corner of Mighell Street. Mothers used to put gates up in case any of the animals escaped, and they never wore red on that day.

I never knew an office worker or anything like that. Most of the girls worked in a laundry and the boys worked on the building sites. You used to see people cleaning shoes on the seafront. You used to see people making alligators and things in the sand, with stones for eyes. But you're not allowed to do things like that now, you'd have to pay for a pitch.

Mount Pleasant

Mount Pleasant and Park Place mid 1930s

The cottages of Mount Pleasant stood for a full century until 1935. Located just down the hill from the imposing gateway into Queen's Park, they were desperately cramped, as the Council report shows. There is still a Mount Pleasant on the site, a steep little hill running up from Eastern Road close to Upper Rock Gardens, but now filled with low rise Council flats and houses.

From the County Borough of Brighton Council Agendas of November 1933:

The Mount Pleasant and Park Place Area is unfit for human habitation.

In Mount Pleasant the total span of the two rows of houses, including the street, is only 58 feet. In the middle of the street the distance from house to facing house is less than fifteen feet. Properties are only 18 feet from front to back and have an average frontage of 12 feet.

The houses on the east side have yards that are mostly 'open', though small. The houses on the west side of the street have no open yards or very small enclosed yards with high walls.

Twenty houses are without sinks

Apollo Terrace

Apollo Terrace was built about 1825, clinging to the hillside. It was a classic example of squeezing in more houses where there should have been none. It disappeared during the huge 1950s redevelopment at the foot of Albion Hill. The Terrace was situated up the steep slope above the third section of today's John Street, which is also called by its old name of Sussex Terrace. On the site today there is only a retaining wall for the street above, still called Elmore Road.

Renee Kelly and Mary Banks jointly talk of their childhood there:

We were born in Apollo Terrace, a street that ran from Sussex Street to Richmond Street, known as 'Polly Alley'. It was very narrow lane, with 37 houses on one side only and a big wall facing us in front to protect from the big drop to Sussex Terrace. That's why it was called an alley, because that's what it was like. When they had the landslide the big wall went right into the back gardens of Sussex Terrace.

The houses in Apollo Terrace were very small, although they didn't seem small when we were little. You went into the front door and straight into the front room, then into the kitchen where there was a flight of stairs up to the two bedrooms. At the back there was a small yard with a big wall protecting us from Elmore Road. We had our toilet in the yard with the tin bath hanging on the wall.

The people in the street were lovely, nice and clean. Mrs Monk belonged to the Salvation Army and Mrs Yandell belonged to the church. Every Christmas Mrs Batchelor had a Christmas party for the children. All the children would go in her house and it was quite a novelty because she had a Christmas tree on the table and all the kids sitting round.

I remember Mr. Laid the milkman coming round with his cart with milk in the churn which he used to ladle out. I often wonder how he got his handcart up that hill with that big churn of milk. It was very steep.

I suppose the area was poor but we were all the same. Our mum used to take her sheets down to pawn them in Edward Street on Mondays all nicely laundered in a paper wrapper, for which she'd get about one or two shillings.

I always used to think that William Street and Henry Street were worse streets. They were rough, especially Henry Street. It had Barnes the salvage firm there and lorries were outside there loading the compressed salvage. There were also a couple of dirty, little houses along there.

There were quite a few pubs in the area but the 'Blue House' (The Lion and Unicorn) was the most noted for being rough. It was called the 'Blue House' because it had blue glass in the windows. The glass has now gone and the woodwork is painted red. When we moved to Kingswood Flats our bedroom faced out towards the pub. Directly we heard fighting on Saturday night we were watching at the window. We had a cabaret every weekend.

We went to Richmond Street Infant's School and then to St John's. We didn't have to go far - fall over twice and you're there.

We used to go to Brighton Girls' Club in Tilbury Place for sixpence a week. It was open every day, but you could only go on Sunday if you attended the little church service in the hall. Miss Prior used to play the organ and had very interesting speakers every week. Her father was very active there as well. She was very posh - she seemed posh to us anyway - but she was lovely as well. She was a big woman with nice shaped legs, and so dainty on her feet when she danced.

We used to have dancing every night when the Juniors went home. It was a very big hall, with fires and couches around the edge where you could sit and do knitting, because there was always a bag of wool, or you could read or play games and puzzles.

There were two huge oil paintings on the walls facing each other. One was of Grace Darling and the other Florence Nightingale and we often wonder what happened to the portraits.

Just before Christmas the table tennis tables were full of old Christmas cards and we would trace them and paint them.

Wednesday night was drama, and we used to be in all the plays and even got on the stage down at the Dome. Thursday night would be 'mixed club' when the boys from the Boys' Club would come up and we'd have dancing. Friday night was PT night (physical training).

When you joined you were put in a certain team and they had captains and vice-captains. The teams had names, but I can only remember Cavell & Nightingale. The captains could go into a little room by the stage, which was their private room and they were allowed to smoke there. There was a canteen, and during the war you could get a penny Oxo drink and a baked potato. It was my life. I went there every night. Well what else was there to do?

Ivory Place

There is an Ivory Place with us still, a narrow, stub, end of a street just to the north of the Municipal Market, with a parking lot on one side and a row of Council houses on the other. The School Clinic has been at the end of the street since the early 1930s. Ivory Place was built as part of the big expansion of the town in the 1820s.

Henry Tullett makes it sound a pleasant place to have lived:

Ivory Place was the home of my paternal grandmother Edith Tullett. She was living there when I was born in 1921, and she stayed on after my grandfather died in 1927 until World War Two. At one point two of my father's older brothers had had to go into the Warren Farm Orphanage for a couple of years, so things must have been difficult for her.

I lived in Ivory Place from 1935 until I joined the Air Force in 1939. It was a little row of houses that sloped down from Richmond Street on the north to Sussex Street on the south, and by today's standards most had nice little gardens. It was a very narrow street with small pavements. At the top end the houses had some very long gardens, and I believe that Gunns, the florist family, used to live in one. Then you came to a row of terraced houses which were without front gardens as they were opposite J J G Saunders' builder's yard which stuck out, but they did have basements. Below that the road widened.

The school clinic and the chest clinic had already been built by 1935, and the Brighton TB Dispensary was at the end of Ivory Place.

My grandmother's house was on the east side and had very small rooms with a very narrow staircase. You'd walk in the front door straight into the front room. There was quite a large yard where grandmother kept her mangle. The house was riddled with bugs because the walls were plastered. There was an alleyway up the side and a big gate that you opened to go into the yard, and then some steps that went up to the back garden. When my grandfather was alive he had a big work shed there. At the back there was a big wall and then Richmond Street School towering over us. In front we had a postage stamp garden with railings round it. Some of the houses had already been demolished when I left. After the war the rest of the street was demolished, but other streets condemned before the war still survive today.

L Boyle also lived in the street and recalls:

I lived in Ivory Place and went to Circus Street School. As we were very poor I cannot remember having any new clothes until I left school and went out to work.

opposite: Ivory Place, between Sussex Street and Richmond Street, demolished 1959

They were funny little houses in the Place, but tidy. We whitened the door step every morning. It was a very friendly street with lots of life. We lived next door to Mrs Gunn who used to sit outside Hanningtons selling violets.

I remember the children sliding down Sussex Street on tin trays when it had snowed.

W Holmes also remembers Ivory Place:

I was born at my grandmother's house in Sussex Terrace on Xmas Eve 1925. The house was full of assorted aunts, uncles and cousins. My family had just one room in the house. Space was at such a premium that my cot was the bottom drawer of a chest-of-drawers. My sister saved me from suffocation once when somebody inadvertently shut the drawer with me in it.

When I was a year old we moved to my other grandparents, in Ivory Place. Grandfather there was a fisherman. Fisherfolk invariably had large families and it was not uncommon for many relatives to have the same Christian names, so nicknames were used based on a person's appearance.

Fishing was a precarious living in those days. The men were away from home much of the time because it was the practice to follow the shoals of herring and mackerel as they moved down the Channel and to land the catches wherever they were. In the meantime the families back in Brighton were living on credit. Sometimes the earnings that were brought back only just covered the credit. Grandfather eventually gave up fishing and worked as a coach painter at Lancing Carriage works.

Rear of Ivory Place

Sussex Street school just before demolition 1962

Sussex Street

Sussex Street ran from the top of the hill down to Grand Parade, following the old leakway between the furlongs. Only the top part remains today, blocked by the 1950s flats.

Richmond Street school opened in 1873. In 1926 it amalgamated with Circus Street school to form Sussex Street schools. It was the first school in Brighton to provide school meals, including breakfasts for its pupils. It even continued to provide food during the school holidays.

Bernard Goldberg recalls:

My father, a coppersmith from Poland, had come to Brighton pre-World War One to repair the roof on the Dome. He stayed on in Brighton and went into sheet metal working and panel beating and eventually had a garage.

I was born at 127 Sussex Street, opposite Ivory Place, where my father had a garage and land that could park about a hundred coaches. They did my father rotten out of the property because he had a Compulsory Purchase Order in 1932 and was offered only the pre-1919 rate for the property. He only got the value of the land and not the

"STAR"
CIRC

buildings or business. Councillor Sherrott tried to help my father, but the other people on the Council were only interested in slum clearance.

It was difficult to find new premises with the small amount of money he was given, but we eventually moved to 15/16 Trafalgar Street which had previously been a slaughterhouse and butchers. It did not have the space for parking coaches. We brought the petrol tank over from Sussex Street and put it in what was called the 'Blood Pit', named from the days when the building was a slaughter house, hence the tiled entrance.

The Goldberg garage survived in Trafalgar Street, just below Sydney Street, until recently. The old tiled signs over the entrance archway remain.

11 Sussex Street 1931 home of David Haywood, barber. 12a - in the foreground - is a confectioner's shop, run by Mrs Ambrose

opposite: Sussex Street c1933. The 'Yacht & Anchor' public house, on the right , is on the corner of Circus Street. The first turning on the left is Ivory Place.

Oxford Court

Oxford Court was a side turning on the south side of Oxford Street. It was an early street though far to the north of most others of the time, being built in the mid 1820s. Street signs to it remain today as it is the parking lot behind the Somerfield store in London Road. The location of some of the original buildings can still be described from the character of the surrounding walls and the lie of the ground.

Benjamin Bowman tells us what it was like to actually live there:

My father, Ernest Bowman, was a boot repairer and he would work all day in the scullery. I remember him sitting at the table with his hammer in his hand and his mouth full of nails. As he used this room the old, black range was never used for cooking by my mother. We had an iron kettle which hung over the fire in the front room, and an old iron gas stove in the scullery for cooking. The scullery had a corrugated roof so that when it rained it made a terrible noise.

My memory of that house was that it was cramped. It was not a shop, but an ordinary house. People would knock on the door to bring or fetch their shoes. All my father's family were in the boot repair business, but I didn't fancy it and never thought of joining my father.

The Oxford Street area was very busy and full of shops. At the top was 'The Bat and Ball' pub (still there, though much rebuilt) and Oxford Place, a narrow lane of very small houses. In Oxford Street there was a hairdresser, a watchmender, a hardware store, a grocer, Tully's the removal people, two cycle shops, a second pub 'The Oxford Arms', Clarke's bread shop, Bellman's the hosiers - who later had the big store around the corner in what is now Somerfield's supermarket - Mrs Ford's confectioners, a jellied eel shop, Pip Perrolli and his ice-cream, the Oxford Street Chapel which is still there, and a tea room on one corner of London Road and the Premier Seed Shop on the other.

Our house was in Oxford Court. Several trades were carried on there. Behind us there was a big area in which the parents of Sidney Bellman had a sack business. Further into the Court there was a slaughter yard. The cattle would be driven down Trafalgar Street from the station, along London Road and into Oxford Street past our house and into the Court. From my bedroom I could see them being killed. Having the slaughter house there encouraged the rats, and with the bugs in the houses that made it a very unhygienic area.

At one time Oxford Court was known as 'The Black Spot of Brighton', and I seem to remember something to do with children dying. The area was fairly poor and it was

opposite: Oxford Court, at 33 Oxford Street 1934

not made any easier by the number of pubs around. There was always fighting after they had been drinking. Ruby Wine had a bad effect on some members of my family. I remember rats being caught in the sewers and released on the Level for the dogs to catch. I believe this was on one of the Bank Holidays.

As a young boy I remember the Saturday market in Oxford Street. It was open until late and had lanterns hanging on the stalls. A wide assortment of things were sold, with a lot of it food. Stalls were set-up right outside our house, just like the market in Upper Gardner Street. The market later moved to the Level, and later still to its present site. Harry Cowley helped to get that set up.

I don't think that my parents were sorry to leave that house because it was so cramped and we never seemed to get rid of the bugs. Sometimes they would come and take the furniture out and fumigate the whole place, but the bugs would always come back.

My mother was pleased when she got notice to move to a new house in Maresfield Road, on the Manor Farm Estate, and I think they settled there quite well. My father got a job with the Parks and Gardens and never did boot repairing again.

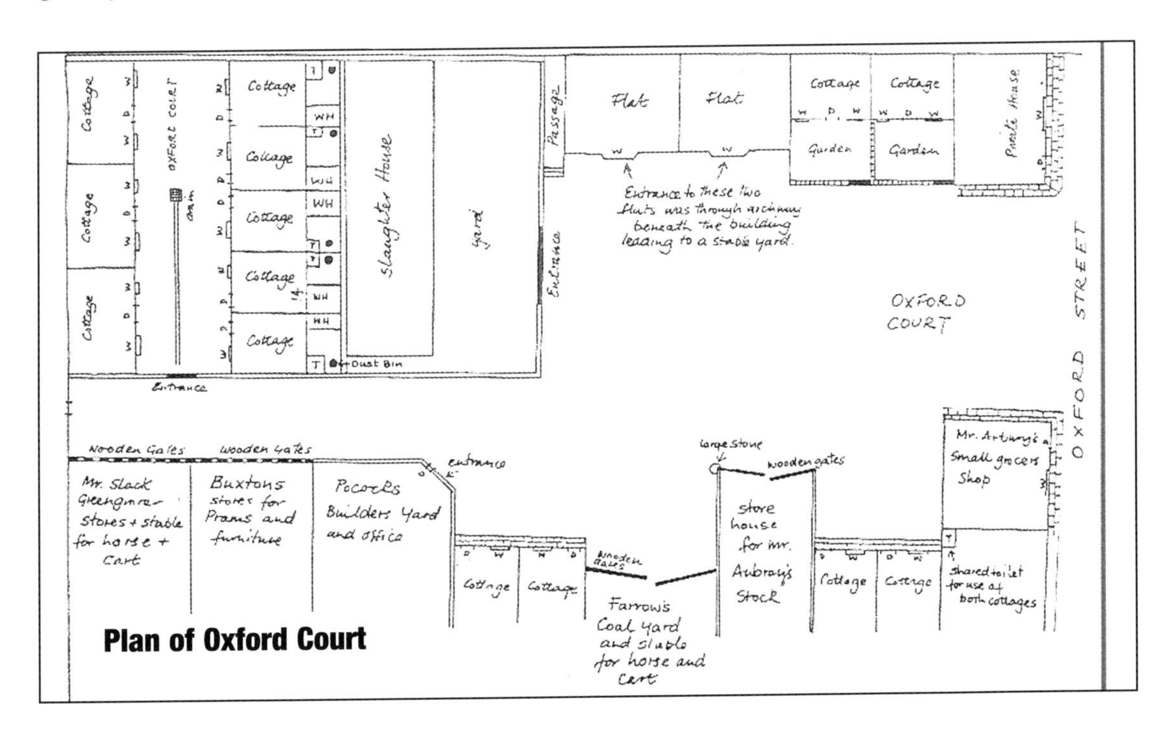

Plan of Oxford Court

opposite: Oxford Court 1934

Ernest Whittington also lived at 14 Oxford Court from 1914 to 1935 with his parents, two brothers and sister Bubbles (Irene). He remembers:

Oxford Court was a little community tucked away behind the London Road, it was rather a quiet place. The houses at the bottom of the Court, where I lived, had a front room and a kitchen with a big coal fire range, used for both cooking and heating. The kitchen was always cheerful and warm in spite of being rather dark due to the wall of the slaughter house being only five feet away and extending right to the top of our roof. A door led out of the kitchen to the wash house and scullery.

One of our favourite jobs as children was to go round all the shops collecting rubbish and then to stoke the boiler in the scullery, pretending we were firemen on the old steam engines.

There were just two bedrooms upstairs and a low attic room with a small window, which we used as a playroom. Our next door neighbours brought up twelve children in one of these little cottages.

The slaughter house was in use for most of the time. We could hear the bleating of sheep and the mooing of cattle, and the shots as the animals were killed - day and night for several days at a time. Then it would be quiet for a week or two.

Farmers would bring their animals (75 to 100 at a time) into Brighton Station by train, drive them through the back streets, down Ann Street, across London Road, along Oxford Street and into Oxford Court. The animals were herded into the bottom end of the cul-de-sac, with two men behind them to stop any escaping while the slaughter house gates were opened to allow a few in at a time. It was bad luck if any resident wanted to get to their front door. The cattle would push their noses against the window and peer into the houses.

On the corner of the entrance to the Court was Mr Arbuary's grocery store. It was a cramped little shop with room for only about two customers at a time. The bread was kept in a tea chest next to the door, and every available space, including the counter, was stacked with boxes. We could buy a halfpenn'orth of salt, which Mr Arbuary cut from a block with a rusty saw. The blocks of salt were kept on a hand cart in the street alongside his shop.

The neighbours were all very friendly and my mother specialised in reading their fortunes in the tea leaves, when they dropped in for a chat and a cup of tea.

From the 'Brighton & Hove Herald', 24th March 1928

FAMILY IN A CONDEMNED HOUSE

A Scandal to Brighton.

Sensational disclosures of the conditions in which a family of six have been living in a condemned house in Oxford Court off Oxford Street were made at an inquest at the Brighton Town Hall on Thursday.

The Borough Coroner was inquiring into the death from laryngitis and measles of a child aged three years and seven months. She was Irene Esme, the daughter of Arthur Cecil Leighton, a furniture porter, of 3 Oxford Court, who is now out of work and in receipt of a 'dole' of £1.

The Coroner said "I have visited a good many poor homes, but I must say I have never visited a place as terrible as this house. It is extraordinary that a town like Brighton should have three cottages without any sanitation except an open closet and there should be no water. The property ought to be pulled down, there is no question of that. I don't know who the landlord is, but I don't think he ought to take rent for them".

Leighton said that he paid 6 shillings a week rent for two rooms – one upstairs and one down. There was no closet in the house. There was a closet attached to a house three doors away; this closet has a water tap outside. Three houses have to use this closet, and the public can use it as well as there is no door to it. He added that the house was condemned two years ago but he had been unable to obtain other accommodation. The bedroom used by the family measures 12 feet long, 8 feet wide and 7 feet high.

Replying to the Coroner Leighton said that a nurse from the Health Department had expressed herself satisfied with the condition of the children. There was nothing wrong with the children until about a week ago. The eldest girl then showed a few spots on her face, and was sent home from school because she had a cold. He did not send for the doctor. On Saturday last he found that the other three children had colds. They were kept in bed, given extra nourishment and rubbed with oil.

On the following Sunday he noticed that the girl Irene was not so well, and had difficulty breathing. On Monday she was worse, and a doctor was sent for. Dr Fraser, who was called, said he should inform the health authorities. Later the Medical Officer of Health arrived but the child was then dead. The other children were sent to the sanatorium.

The Medical Officer said that when he was called to the house he saw that it was in a deplorable state. "I went upstairs and found three children lying in the bed. They were obviously ill. The eldest child of the three was desperately ill and dying. I was of the opinion that she was suffering from laryngitis and measles. Between two and three o'clock in the afternoon I found the child lying dead beside the youngest child and the second child appeared to be worse."

Preece's Buildings

There is nothing left of Preece's Buildings, built in the 1820s save a narrow, blind alley in Church Street. The Buildings was one of the earliest infill developments, squeezed into the spaces between streets, so characteristic of Backyard Brighton.

Victor Cox was obviously one of those who were glad to move away and recalls:

My parents were Romanys and lived all over Sussex before they settled in Preece's Buildings. My father was a horse trader, but my parents had a horse and cart and were selling coke when my mother decided that she'd had enough and wanted to settle in a house. The occupant of 7 Preece's Buildings must have known my parents, as she told them that number 6 was going to be empty. My parents went to the landlord. They got the house, on the condition that they decorated it, for a rent of five shillings a week.

I was the first child in the family to be born in a house. My father became a labourer and a scaffolder, and took what work he could get. My mother went out cleaning in a house in Powis Square and in two pubs.

Our house had three floors, was cobbled outside and had only one small room on each floor, about eight feet by nine feet square. The top room was even smaller as it had a sloping roof. As you came in the stairs were straight in front of you. The downstairs room was the only room to live and cook in. My mother cooked on the fire and the black grate by the side of the fire.

We had no back door and no yard, as our house joined the cork factory which supplied the cork shop in Gardner Street. We would lie awake at night and hear the machinery going. There was only one way in and out of the house, through the front door. My mother lived until she was ninety-seven and often said we could have been burnt alive.

We didn't have much furniture in the downstairs room, only a table and kitchen chairs. There was just room to pull the chairs out and sit down at the table, so you can see how small it was. When the coalman came to put the coal under the stairs he had to open the door to this room and we had to move the table over to make space. On the first floor was my parents' bedroom, but you couldn't light a fire there because it would have set the bed alight it was so close.

To reach the top floor you had to mount a curved staircase - where we children slept in two beds, 'top and tailed'. The room was very cold. We never had a light even when gas mantles were put into the other rooms, and we continued to go to bed by candle light until we left the house in 1936. Until 1927 the only lights in the house were oil lamps and candles.

opposite: Preece's Buildings, at 103 Church Street, looking north

As there was no backyard we had no running water. You had to go out of the house just to get a glass of water. Each house had its own wc, but we had to share the wash house. The women used the wash house in a rota system. I think my mother had use of it on Monday or Tuesday. When the clothes were clean they were rinsed and put on one of the lines across the street. I don't remember there ever being any rows about the rotas or the use of the lines. When we came home from school on Mondays and Tuesdays we had to dodge in and out of the washing to get to our front doors. If it was wet the washing would be draped over lines inside the house which was not pleasant.

Our neighbours stayed the same for years and I can still remember who lived in each house. Two of them were fishermen who had boats on the beach. Before Good Friday they would be cleaned for the trippers and used as pleasure boats.

Everyone helped each other in those days. We didn't have much, and it was hand to mouth existence, but everyone was the same. Sometimes the rent money would be late and I would have the job of taking it round to the landlord. If kids were ill the neighbours would rally round and help. There were arguments amongst the adults, but this was only to be expected living on top of each other and they were short lived rows. Generally all the kids got on.

In 1936 my parents were told they were going to be rehoused as Preece's Buildings were to be demolished. They were quite happy to go as they had no amenities there.

Manor Farm was the area we were to be moved to and I went with my father to look at the estate. The houses were like Buckingham Palace compared with Preece's Buildings, having running water, a bathroom, plenty of living and sleeping space and electric light with just a switch. They also came with an electric cooker with the Corporation crest on it and an electric kettle. My mother was always afraid of electricity and didn't want to use them.

We had a lovely view up there, not like at Preece's Buildings where we looked out of the downstairs room onto a high brick wall with ladders and barrows. My parents were very happy with their new house. I didn't see much of the children I knew after we moved because the war started. Some were killed but many moved away.

A Lambert also lived in the Buildings and remembers:

My parents were tenants in Preece's Buildings in the 1930s, a cul-de-sac between Gardner Street and Regent Street with a narrow entrance in Church Street. There were approximately ten cottages and two communal wash houses on the left hand side of the lane, with the toilets opposite the houses and backing onto the buildings in Regent Street. There were no gardens or bathrooms, so most people used the public baths in North Road. Most of the children attended the Central School in Regent Street, which also had an entrance in Church Street facing New Road.

opposite: Preece's Buildings looking south to the entrance from Church Street

101 North Street

This house was tucked into a small close directly across from Wykeham Terrace at the bottom of Dyke Road. Today it lies under Century House, which still juts out into the road near the Clock Tower bus stop in Dyke Road, just as the old close did.

From the thesis of R Grant on 'Public Health in Brighton'.

From the 1867 sewage map I can exactly locate the fisherman and the white-washed windows. A social note is provided by the broom. How clean and tidy the yard is. It is likely the fisherman ran his home like he ran his ship, all ship-shape and Bristol fashion. Although the photo suggests poverty, there is also a touch of pride in this man who has made the best of what little he has.

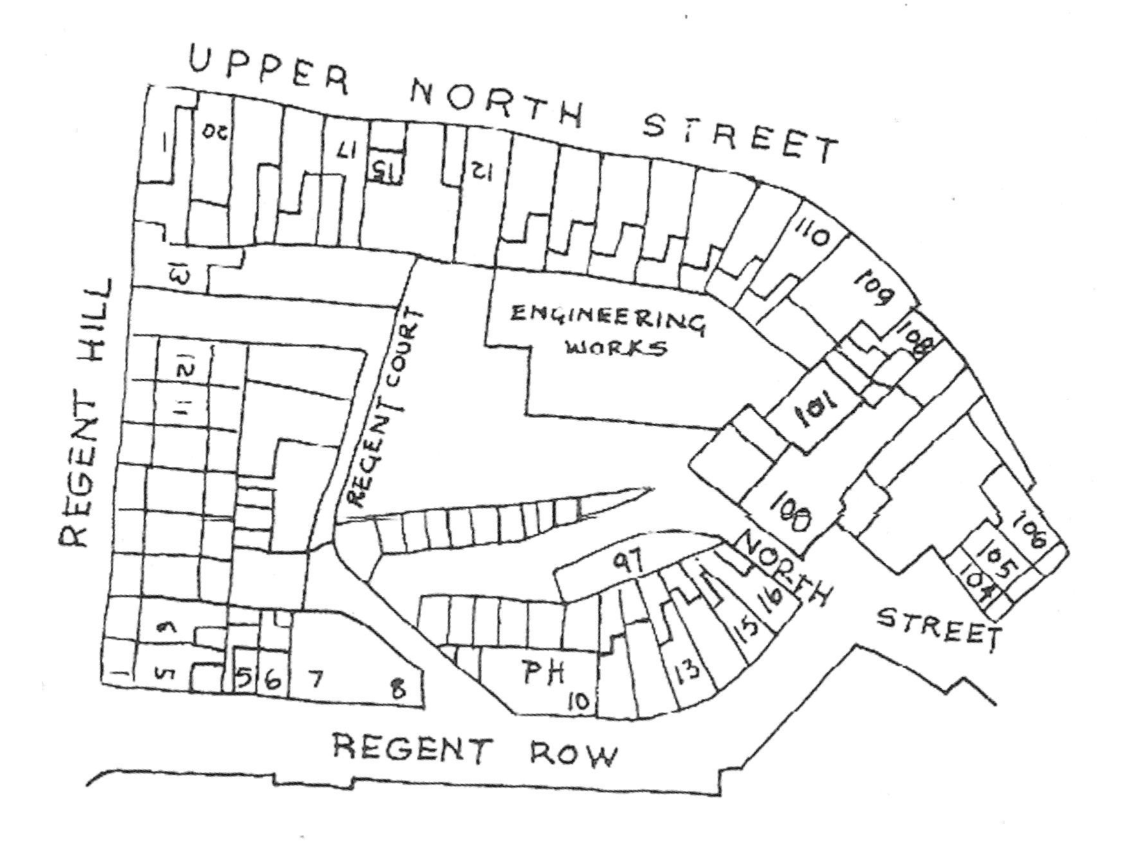

opposite: 101 North Street mid 1930s

Russell Place

Russell Place was part of the early development to the west of the Old Town, being created in the 1820s. There is still a Russell Place, tucked as a blank-walled cul-de-sac into the side of the parking lots behind Churchill Square.

Albert Lewis argues very firmly that it was a better place to live than it appeared.

I have lovely memories of the area. I lived in a fisherman's cottage and, though everyone was poor, there was a camaraderie that does not exist today. Each mother instilled wonderful discipline in her kids and made sure you were honest. We were scrupulously clean and well turned out, and we got a very good basic education at Middle Street School.

Once we had no food in the house at all and I had to go for a meal to the soup kitchen in Southover Street, a long way to traipse there and back for a small boy. They treated you like the scum of the earth at the kitchen. I vowed never to go back, and I never did.

We used to hate Sundays. We had a special set of clothes kept for that day, and had to go to church at St Paul's nearby and Sunday School.

opposite: Russell Place 1935 with St Paul's church in the background

Sun Street

Sun Street was wedged between William Street and Colonnade Mews that was further down the hill towards the Steine. It had three storey houses on one side and the blank backs of the yards of William Street on the other. Today it lies under the building formerly known as the Art College, and Civil Courts buildings at the bottom of Edward Street. Sun Street was described in Council reports as 'very badly lit and an example of the bad arrangement of buildings'.

Dorothy Farrell gives us a more graphic view of the place:

Sun Street was a small lane and the people who lived there seemed to be poorer, some of them seemed to be like gypsies. They would sit on their steps outside and talk. When we went to the beach the lads used to say 'Let's go through Sun Street', but my mum said never to go through Sun Street because of the terrible things that happened there like bad language and razor gangs, but of course we never saw anything.

From the 'Brighton & Hove Herald' 21 January 1928.

I understand that Brighton Corporation are contemplating condemning as unhealthy a large number of dwelling houses in the Sun Street of Brighton, and invoking the aid of the Housing Act, 1925 for the purposes of compulsorily acquiring the property in the area.

I wonder how many members of the Town Council have any idea of the gross injustice which is inflicted upon property owners by the town taking the advantage of the powers given them by this iniquitous Act.

The total compensation payable to the unfortunate owner may be less than the site value of the land, irrespective of the value of any building which may be upon it. This would amount to an infinitesimal sum compared to the cost of the property to the owner. The amount of a mortgage is ignored entirely, with the result that in almost every case the amount of compensation payable is very much less than the amount which is due to the mortgagees of the property. In many cases, persons of small means are dependent for their livelihood upon incomes from such properties, and which have been purchased out of a life's savings.

I wonder if the members of the Brighton Town Council are aware that a Committee, of which Mr Nevill Chamberlain was chairman, has promised to amend the basis of compensation for premises acquired under Section 46 of the Housing Act, 1925. Whilst I appreciate the activities of the Brighton Corporation to improve our town, surely this should not be done at the expense of a small number of ratepayers whose only crime is that they have invested their savings in small property. 'Fair Play'

From the 'Brighton & Hove Herald' 28 January 1928

Alderman Black suggested that some properties have been bought quite recently at 'knock-down prices', with the knowledge of the coming condemnation. Mr Cane declared that the desire to clear this property was prompted not by the desire desire to put other houses on the site for the working classes, but to have an open space which could be used for garaging cars.

opposite: Sun Street, between Edward Street and Carlton Hill, built 1800-1808

Gloucester Terrace

Gloucester Terrace was another of the infill buildings erected in the 1830s, and is today underneath the recently renovated terraced Council housing on the north side of Gloucester Street. There is no visible sign of it, or of the nearby Gloucester Cottages which were home to the redoubtable Granny Smith.

L Scarborough gives us a colourful picture of life in Gloucester Terrace:

Gloucester Terrace consisted of ten similar houses in a cul-de-sac. There were small gardens and a narrow brick path outside the houses. Open the front door and on the right was the front room, which we were only allowed to go into on a Sunday, and then only if we sat and read a book, or played Ludo, Putt & Take, or Snakes and Ladders.

Behind was a kitchen-cum-living room with a big range that had to be black leaded every day, and above was a cupboard used to air the clothes. There were also two cupboards next to each other, one for china and food and the other for coal. If you happened to be having a meal when the coalman called, you had to get up from the table and move the chairs so the coalman could put the coal in. Apart from the table and wooden chairs there was a chiffonier, or sideboard as they are called now. Under the window was a black horse hair sofa that used to scratch the back of our legs when we sat on it unless we had a blanket on it.

You were considered well off if you had a wireless. We didn't, but we did have a wind-up gramophone with a big horn and about six records. We learned most of the new songs from the errand boys, who would go round on their bikes whistling them. You could always tell a new errand boy as they wore short trousers. After they had been at work a few weeks they earned enough money to buy their first pair of long trousers. My brother got his first pair of long trousers on his fourteenth birthday, but was only allowed to wear them on Sunday until he left school.

The lavatory was at the bottom of the yard. It had a pull chain but the seat was just a large wooden plank with a hole in it which went from wall to wall. One of our jobs on a Saturday morning if it was wet was to sit at the table after breakfast and cut up squares of newspaper. Then we made a hole in the corner and threaded string through to hang up for toilet paper. In those days the print didn't come off like it does now.

The stairs were very dark and a gas jet at the bottom always had to be lit before anyone went up them. There were gas jets downstairs with white mantles, but no lighting upstairs so we used candles with large enamel candle holders. There were three bedrooms upstairs, a front one and two small ones at the back for each boy. The front one was shared by my mother and grandmother. My bedroom had a double iron bed, with brass bedknobs which my brother and I used to unscrew and leave notes for one another when we were old enough to write. There was a cupboard that held our clothes, and a marble washstand with a jug and basin - not that we ever washed upstairs because it would have made work carrying water upstairs. In the winter we washed in a bowl on the kitchen table and in the summer we washed in the scullery sink. We had a chamber pot under the bed, as it was too dark and cold to go downstairs and out into the yard at night.

We had no heating upstairs, but we thought we were lucky as we had a stone hot water bottle each. There was no bathroom, but we had a long tin bath that hung on a nail in the yard and it was brought in every Friday in front of the fire. You had to be very careful in the bath as the side facing the door was cold but the side by the fire was very hot, so if you happened to touch the side you either froze or burnt. After our baths we were given a dose of Syrup of Figs whether we needed it or not.

When we were about twelve years old we were considered too old to bath in front of the fire, so we used run errands for old people or clean front steps for a halfpenny and by Saturday we had earned about thruppence, so we used to go to North Road Baths, and have a bath there for two pennies. Mum used to give us a penny and with the money we had over we would go to the silent films. We got in for two pence, which included a bag of unshelled peanuts and we sat on forms ankle deep in peanut shells.

We always had new sandals at Whitsun. They had leather tops with crepe soles. They cost two and eleven a pair, and were always bought half a size too big, as they had to last all summer. If they wore out before August we had to make do with a shilling pair of plimsolls instead. Before we went back to school after the August holiday we would have a new pair of black, lace-up shoes that had to last us all winter. They had leather soles and uppers, and if they wore out the boot repairer would repair them in two hours unless he was very busy. He used to charge two and sixpence to repair a pair of men's boots, two shillings for ladies and one and six for children, and an extra threepence for boys. If they had what we used to call horse shoes on the heels (a piece of steel shaped like a horse shoe set into the heel) it saved the boys wearing down the heels so quickly. I used to envy the boys because they could strike their heels on the pavement and make sparks.

Going up Gloucester Street a bit further there was Gloucester Cottages, and in a house at the end of the alley lived a lady called Granny Smith. Every set of streets had an old lady that people went to for help looking after the family when a baby was due. In those days you didn't go to hospital to have a baby unless you were rich. You had your baby at home, with a midwife in attendance. Large families were normal, many having a child every year. My mother finished up having nine by her second husband. It was also not uncommon for two or three to die before reaching school age.

Granny Smith would come in and look after my mother and the children, cook the dinner and do the washing for a tanner a day and her dinner. When the father came in from work he was expected to take over, so on Sundays Granny Smith only worked if a

Gloucester Street, between Gloucester Place and Sydney Street, 1935

baby was born on that day. Some people were so poor they didn't have any sheets on the bed and they were ashamed to let the midwife see they had no sheets, so Granny Smith would loan them a pair for three pence a week.

If anybody was ill you called Granny Smith in, as she had a lot of homemade remedies. You had to be almost dying before you saw the doctor because it cost a shilling. If you were well enough to go to the surgery you weren't sick enough for the doctor to visit. That cost two and sixpence and you had to pay him first before he would look at the person who was ill. Of course there was always the Parish Doctor, but you could only have him after they had been into what money you had coming in, what they call a Means Test. Even then you had to pay a bit towards the medicine.

Granny Smith would also lay people out when they died. Everybody kept a starched white nightdress, or for a man a nightshirt, wrapped in paper for their funeral. Granny Smith would charge a shilling to lay a body out, as in those days the funeral parlour used to charge more. She would wash the body, close the eyes by putting pennies on the lids and dress them in their funeral clothes.

Although people couldn't help being poor, it was looked upon as a disgrace if you had a pauper's funeral, which meant a plain horse and cart would come and take the body away in a plain, unvarnished box. Most people would pay about a penny or two a week into a funeral club. Thruppence a week would cover a mother, father and up to six children. Funerals cost about £3 for the hearse and consisted of a black carriage pulled by two black horses adorned with big, black plumes. The relations followed behind on foot. The price of a funeral included a polished coffin. People either side of the house where the person had died would pull their curtains closed as a sign of respect, and men in the street would take off their caps until the coffin had passed. I used to love to watch a funeral with the horses and their long black plumes and the men in frock coats and their top hats. If a wife lost her husband she wore black for a year, and then went mauve half-mourning for another year.

When Granny Smith wasn't working she would make lovely toffee apples, a halfpenny for one and a penny for two. She would also lend money if you were hard up. She would lend you half a crown, and when you paid her back you would give her two shillings, eight and half pence - a penny in the shilling interest. There used to be a rumour going around that she had stacks of money in her cottage, but she never refused to help anybody, even if at the time they couldn't pay her. But it was a matter of principle to pay her later.

My mother never did her weekend shopping until 6 o'clock on Saturday evening, as the butchers didn't have fridges in those days and they would start selling the meat off cheap. There were two butchers in Sidney Street next to one another and they would vie with each other. For two and sixpence mother would either get a big joint of beef or a whole leg of lamb. Then she had the cheek to say 'I want something to cook it with', so the butcher would give her a lump of fat free. We used to have lovely dripping on Mondays from the joint. She would go up to Upper Gardner Street and get 14lb. of potatoes for a shilling, two large cabbages for three pence and half a carrier of what we called pot veg for sixpence - carrots, onions, parsnips, turnips or whatever was in season. Most people had cold meat on Monday with bubble and squeak The only food I remember being in tins was pineapple, sardines and biscuits at Christmas.

Being the eldest girl I had to go with Mum to help carry the shopping home. For this I would get a halfpenny cornet in summer and a pennyworth of hot chestnuts from the man at the corner of Kensington Gardens in winter, with instructions to eat up before I got home and don't tell the others as she couldn't afford to buy for all of us. Ever tried eating a cornet carrying two bags of shopping?

Saturday night was our treat night. Mother and Gran went to the market in Upper Gardner Street and they used to stay there until about nine o'clock at night. When it was dark they used to tie flaming torches on to the barrows. Mum or Gran would bring us back fish and chips, a tuppenny piece of fish and a penn'orth of chips each, and a tuppenny bottle of lemonade between my brother and me.

Everybody had fly papers hanging up in those days. These were needed as there were a lot of flies. The papers were a penny each and when you bought them they were in a roll with a bit of string on top. You held them over heat, and as they got warm you pulled them out and hung them up in the house. They were sticky and the flies were attracted to them.

When the men were out of work families had to go on Relief, which meant somebody from the Council would come to your house to see if you had anything you could sell. So if a neighbour had to go on Relief they would knock on your door and say 'The Relief man is coming, can you look after a few bits for me?'. No one ever refused and in would come the treasures, probably only worth a few shillings but worth much more to the owners. The Relief man would give them vouchers for groceries and coal - five shillings worth for each adult, and three shillings for each child. They never gave money in case it was spent in the pub. People used to get a little bit of dole money, just enough to pay the rent and put money in the gas meter. We used to welcome the gas man because Mum always got a rebate which meant we got a treat, either jelly and cream for tea or fish and chips for supper.

If children needed clothes, they were given a card to take to the clinic in Prince's Street, where there was a room with second-hand clothes. You would be given one of everything, like one vest, etc. I don't know what children were supposed to wear while these clothes were washed.

We did not look upon ourselves as being poor, as the poor people had no lino on their floors, only bare boards. When my father was killed in the war, Mother and Grandmother had very little money. My Grandmother was getting seven and sixpence widow's pension. My Mother got a little more as she was a war widow. She got ten shillings for herself and seven and six for my brother, as he was the eldest child, and five shillings for me. Their total income was thus one pound ten shillings for a week. Out of this they had to pay twelve shillings rent, which included rates, two and six for a hundredweight and a half of coal, and fourpence a day for gas, leaving only thirteen and tuppence for food and clothes.

Finding it hard to manage, it was decided that my Grandmother would look after us while my Mother went out to work. She got a job as a tram conductor at ten shillings a week, later being promoted to tram driver at twelve and six a week.

The police used to come round the streets two or three times a day on foot, and if a constable saw a child misbehaving he would clip them round the ear with his gloves. You daren't tell your Mum, as she would only say you must have been doing something to deserve it. The sort of thing you would get a clip for was climbing a lamppost or putting the light on or chalking on the wall. Children were better behaved in those days. We were taught to respect our parents, and if you answered a teacher back you would get a ruler across your knuckles.

We used to go to Sunday School every Sunday and my brother was in the choir, for which he got two and sixpence every three months, and if he sang at a wedding he would get an extra shilling. Our big treat was the Sunday School Outing. For weeks before we would save up a few pence and each grandmother would give us a penny to spend. We had to take our own dinner, which was usually corned beef or jam sandwiches and a bottle of drink which was usually a halfpennyworth of lemonade powder put into a bottle of water. We also had to take an enamel mug with our name sewn around the handle.

We would meet at St Peter's church and march up Trafalgar Street to the station, where we would get a train to the Hassocks Tea Gardens. The swings were free, but the other rides were a halfpenny or a penny. At four o'clock a whistle would blow when we would all rush to the trestle tables at one end of the garden. They would come round with big pots of tea with the milk and sugar already in it and fill our mugs, followed by the sandwiches which were always strawberry jam. Then they would come round with the cakes, which were a halfpenny currant bun and a penny iced cake each. After tea you could go and play, and there was always a rush for the free swings as everybody had spent their money by then. At six o'clock another whistle would blow and we would line up to make sure nobody was missing and be marched to Hassocks Station to catch the train home. I suppose we must have had some wet days on our Treat, but I can only remember one and that didn't happen until we were coming home.

I started school at Pelham Street School when I was five years old. It was a big school, with separate entrances for Infants, Juniors, and Boys and Girls. Infants and Juniors didn't wear uniform. The Senior boys had to wear caps and ties in the school colours of green and yellow; the girls wore navy blue tunics summer and winter, the only difference being they wore white blouses with green and yellow ties in the summer and green jumpers in the winter. There were no school dinners in those days; every child had to go home at dinner time. School hours were from nine until twelve o'clock, then from two until four o'clock for Infants and Juniors and four-thirty for Seniors.

We didn't have books and pencils but slates and chalk, and when we wanted to clean them we had to go to the teacher who would look at what you had written and then give you a damp sponge to wipe your slate. Most of our work was learnt by repetition. Teacher would write something on the blackboard, then we all had to say it out loud as teacher pointed to it. When she thought we knew it, she would rub it off the board and pick a child to stand up and say it. We had the same teacher for all our lessons. You only got a new teacher when you went up a class.

I had only been to school two months when I caught scarlet fever, which in those days was a killer disease as they had no antibiotics. I was taken to hospital at nine o'clock at night, which was like the middle of the night to me. My mother had to have my room fumigated, as well as my clothes, as it was very contagious. I was put into the Fever Hospital, which was at the top of Bear Road, and I was not allowed any visitors. My mother and grandmother had to stand outside and look through the window. At the height of the illness I went blind for three days. I can remember sitting up in the cot screaming that I couldn't see. They put me in a small room and pulled the blinds so

that the light wouldn't hurt my eyes. After three days my sight started coming back and I started getting better. Eventually I was allowed home, but was very weak and not allowed back to school for some time, and then on condition that I didn't do any drill, as PE was called in those days, or run and play games. If only they had seen what I used to get up to when I was playing with the other children!

We played games according to the season. At Easter it was skipping and hoops. It took at least five of us to play the Easter skipping game; we would cross the ropes with one girl at each end, two standing on the opposite pavements, and two in the road. We could always hear the horse and carts coming, and get out of their way in time. We used to run in when the ropes were being turned and the others used to chant a rhyme, at the end of the rhyme we had to run out. At Whitsun it was top-and-whip and marbles. The boys used to play marbles in the gutters, which were quite clean as the road sweeper came round every morning and swept the gutters, and after him would come the water cart, even in the small side streets.

Most of our amusements were homemade, for example four wheelers for the boys consisted of a wooden soap box, a plank of wood, a piece of rope and four wheels off an old pram. The only ready-made amusements were the swings and slides on the Level. As soon as you were eight you joined the Cubs if you were a boy, or the Brownies if a girl. You didn't have any choice, you were told to go by your parents and you went. You never thought of disobeying them.

Park Place

Park Place today consists of some low rise Council flats facing a row of lock-up garages behind the upper part of of Egremont Place. Despite being so close to such stylishness they were particularly bad buildings that were rushed up during the 1830s.

From the Agenda of the County Borough of Brighton Council, 30 November 1933

Park Place Area unfit for human habitation .

These houses open into a forecourt eighteen feet deep which leads into a concrete paved inclined passageway 5 foot wide. Some have basement rooms entirely underground. Two of these basement rooms were in use for sleeping in November 1933. There is one room each on the ground and first floors. Two of the houses are being used as shops – the room on the ground floor has been partitioned off with the front portion used for a shop and the back as the living room. In these cases the living room is so small (7 feet 3 inches x 7 feet 9 inches) that one has to move furniture before being able to approach the staircase. The rooms in the houses have damp, cold walls. The back walls are mostly of brick-bats, and when built were continued up from an old garden wall.

opposite 22 Park Place, between Edward Street and Queen's Park Road, 1935

Gerard's Court at 41 King Street c1935

Gerard's Court

Like Gloucester Terrace, Gerard's Court was part of the 1830s uncontrolled development in which small pieces of unused land were made to bear rows of tiny cottages cheek by jowl. Today it lies under the large Church Street multistorey car park.

Bert Nelson remembers the small Court with warmth and affection:

I lived at number 1 Gerard's Court with my parents and grandparents from my birth in 1927 until we were moved in 1936. My grandfather, George Dann, had been a fisherman all his working life and fished in his own vessel from Brighton beach. A hardy and weatherbeaten old salt, he lived well into his eighties in spite of smoking dark, coarse, uncut shag tobacco in his many long, clay 'churchwarden' pipes.

My grandmother was a formidable soul, well built as seemed to be the way of things in those days. I can still remember her daily striding up the passage which led to King Street and returning gingerly with a quart jug filled to the brim with dark stout.

Gerard's Court, or the Court as we called it, was bounded on three sides with houses, the fourth and west side being formed by a wall which to a youngster seemed to be enormously high. This wall played a prominent part in our lives. It could almost be termed our Olympic Stadium, for against it we would throw balls, play cricket and football, run against it and jump at it, we would chalk on it and ride tricycles and scooters at it.

Gerard's Court could be entered by passages from both King Street and Church Street. The passage from Church Street had three or four cottages along it, but they were not counted as belonging to the Court.

The passage from King Street was about 20 feet long and 5 feet wide. Houses in King Street backed onto The Court and the backs of their yards formed our high wall. The houses on the north side of The Court were faced with pebbles - not any of your little, namby-pamby pebbles, but good large, round, ones - cobbles I suppose - about three to four inches in diameter. These were symmetrically placed in the manner of bricks, and formed an extremely durable building.

Houses on the eastern side were rendered and scored to look like blocks. I recall our house as having three floors and that access to the upper floors was by a narrow and enclosed, twisting wooden staircase. Lighting was by gas lamp, paraffin lamp or even a candle.

We had a front parlour, used only on Christmas Eve, or to allow for the laying out of the body of anyone in the family who died. The parlour had a black leaded open fireplace with a high mantel decorated by an overhanging cloth with fluffy bobbles. The woodwork was dark brown and the embossed wallcovering was also a dark shade.

In those days wallcoverings were pasted to the wall with a flour and water mix, which was just about adequate but not easy to use. It was also the fashion to clear varnish the covering once it was in position, making it one heck of a job to remove. I recall that my grandfather, having made an extremely good job of preparing the hallway, then proceeded to varnish it with brown varnish so that the hallway was always really gloomy after that.

Our yard was small, maybe fifteen foot by four, and contained at one end the wc. It was tiny with whitewashed walls and a wooden door with a gap at the top and bottom. The 'seat' was a wooden plank with a hole cut in it. A candle stub was required, and whatever paper was available cut into squares and hung up. In the depths of winter and on wet dark nights this was not the place to be, but since we children were always dosed with Syrup of Figs in order that we should 'go', trips were a necessity.

Trips outside the Court were few, mostly to attend school, first as infants in Upper Gardner Street and then to the Central School in Church Street. Our shopping for food was done at Stenning's the grocers on the west side of King Street near the entrance of the Court. We would leave a list of our needs which could then be collected or delivered. The milkman would arrive daily pushing a cart containing tall, gleaming churns of milk festooned with shiny, metal, measuring jugs. His appearance would be announced by a cacophony of sound from his jangling jugs. People would arrive with their own jugs and bear them carefully away to be placed on the stone slab in the cool larder, covered with a piece of lace or muslin edged with shiny glass beads to weigh it down and form a cap.

Probably the only technical device in the home was the radio, which provided reason for another expedition from the Court. These radios were powered by 'accumulators', which were glass containers of acid carried by a handle. They would need recharging, and we would be entrusted with taking them to a garage in King Street, being warned as to the dire consequences of dropping the device. We were not only being allowed out of The Court, we were also being instructed to enter 'The Garage'. At this time there were few motor vehicles and I cannot recall seeing any in that garage.

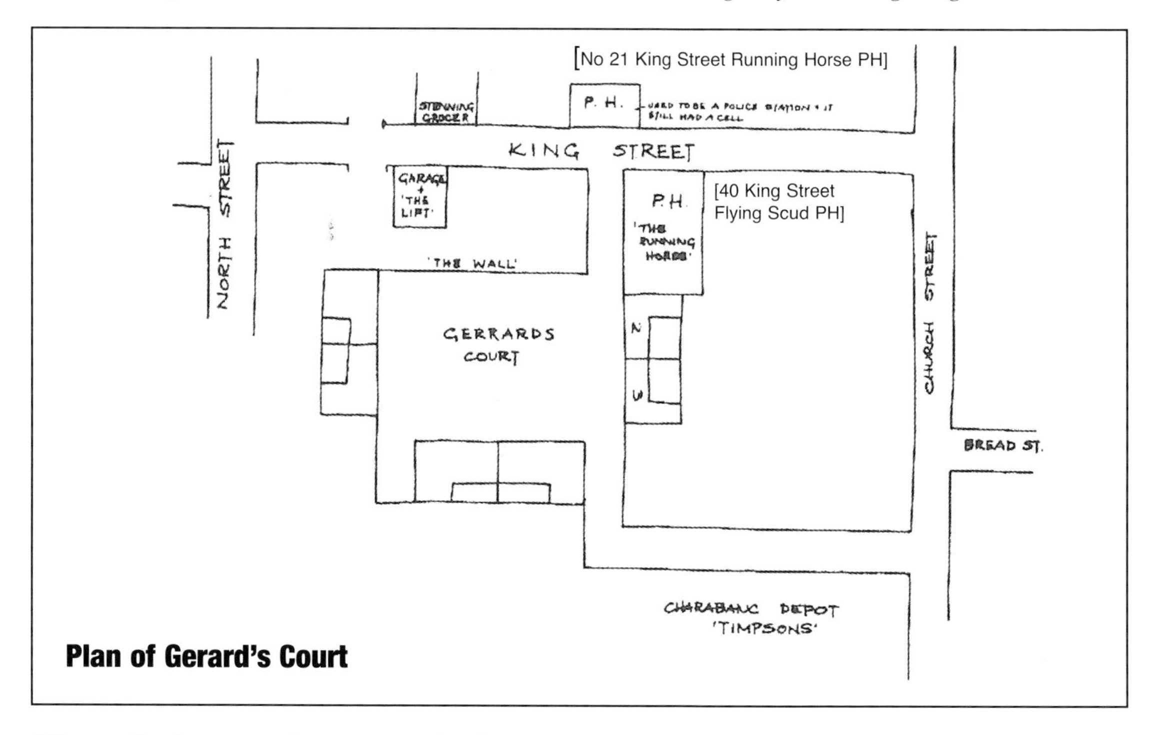

Plan of Gerard's Court

The real adventure for us was the heart thumping, eye-popping sight of 'The Lift'. This was a goods lift, large enough to transport motor vehicles and we would ride it to the top floor, two or three floors up. One might ask what all the fuss was about over a ride in a lift, but in our kind of lifestyle this was the ultimate. This thrill of 'The Lift' never left us, no matter how many times we did the trip.

King Street was an extension of our playground. There we would play 'whip-to-top', whipping and twirling our wooden tops with much gusto, and here also would propel our hoops of wood up and down the street shouting and squealing. Another game which was popular was 'alleys' - glass marbles, multi-coloured and much coveted. The so-called 'blood alleys' were the most prized, which were white with swirls of red through them. We would bring out our drawstringed 'alley bags', which we had coaxed our mothers to make from any piece of highly patterned cloth, and troop into King Street to play up and down the gutters with cries of pleasure or dismay. Occasionally an alley would roll down into somebody's 'area', a grating-covered space in front of houses intended to allow light into the basement room. Someone who was in favour with his mother at that time would be persuaded to return home and beg the use of the clothes prop and a piece of soap. A quick hoist of the prop and the alley would be retrieved.

King Street would also provide its own free entertainment every evening. The street lamps were, of course, gas lamps, and there was much running up and down the street when the lamp lighter was due. He would appear on his bicycle, riding one-handed and bearing in his other hand the lamp lighting pole. With not a pause in the pace of his ride he would deftly prod the switch on the top of the lamppost and 'pop', the lamp would splutter into life. He earned the applause and shouts that greeted each successful encounter, though I doubt he enjoyed the attention.

Another thrill we enjoyed was 'watching'. On the Church Street side was an extremely large garage, used to house charabancs. I believe the name of the coach firm was Timpson's. We would stand and gaze for many an hour at these gleaming monsters, smelling the distinctive fumes as they were shunted back and forth. What far places did they visit? How privileged the passengers were!

If we behaved and attended Sunday School regularly we could become one of these privileged people and enjoy a ride in one of these craft. This annual event would be a visit to a place outside our world, to Hassocks, and it would ensure that for weeks in advance there was much good behaviour. After a noisy and boisterous journey out, lots of rides on toy motor cars, swings, slides and roundabouts and a free sit-down tea, the ride back was much quieter, with sleepy heads and not a few queasy tummies. Roll on next year!

I recall life in The Court as one of utter bliss. It seems we had only long, hot summers - perhaps an illusion, but life there was magic. The Court seemed to be all protecting and we were a little colony not caught up in the outside world. We lived our lives there, we played there, it was our entire world. I cannot recall any intolerance and, considering the very close proximity we had, the harmony seemed unbroken. In our little world we had comfort, peace and security. That is a child's viewpoint of Gerard's Court. An adult's would embrace the grim economics of an existence where wages were low and social services non-existent.

For me Gerard's Court was a Utopia. I still love the memory of it. When I am in the vicinity of King Street those ghosts can still draw me back to those lovely, warm childhood days.

LYONS' TEA
LYONS' TEA
LYONS TEA
TIZER
TIZER

Carlton Hill

Star Tavern outing 1928 in Grand Parade

Lou Morris, owner of the boarding house in William Street, shown on page 26, is in front of the above photograph with his accordion. Some of the children have bare feet.

From the 'Brighton & Hove Herald' 16th February 1924

As a ratepayer and tradesman of Brighton for the past fifty years I was compelled by old age to give up business and found the greatest difficulty in obtaining a small house in which to reside with my family.

However at last I bought a small, four-roomed cottage which was built about one hundred years ago. It is situated in the great slum district of Carlton Hill, and has no yard or garden, nor any usual household conveniences. Such a cottage would not now be allowed to be built by the Corporation.

There are about twelve similar slum cottages in the same condition in one road, and they are occupied in most instances by several families in each house, thus destroying all privacy and real home life. This overcrowding is mainly caused by the excessive rate assessment of these slums by our local Guardian's Assessment Committee and their officers. Their policy seems to consist of raising the assessments of these slum cottages and so compelling the poor tenants to pay such high rentals that they are forced to herd together as cattle, without regard to health or decency.

I gave £100 for my cottage (freehold), and the assessment for rates is £10. The past year's rates and taxes are over four shillings alone. Tenants are compelled to pay a rental (inclusive) of ten to twelve shillings weekly. I have placed my protest before the Guardian's Committee against my excessive assessment. Their reply is they cannot reduce it, and as ratepayers we have no power to remedy this state of things, but simply go as lambs to the slaughter and pay. **'Carlton'**

opposite: 91 Carlton Hill, E A Corder general store, on the corner of William Street

Edwin Place, Montague Place to Upper Bedford Street

Edwin Place

Edwin Place was a lane running parallel to Eastern Road on its south side at Upper Bedford Street. Nowadays it is lost underneath an eighties development mix of sheltered housing and high rise Council flats across the road from the Industrial Estate, on the site of the old Kemp Town Station.

Gladys Stenning tells us it was a pretty place with pleasant front gardens and houses that in these times would be much sought-after cottages:

Edwin Place was a pretty little street. I lived at number four with my mother, father and sister until I was sixteen when we had to move because of redevelopment. Our house had two bedrooms, parlour, kitchen and an outside wc. There was no bathroom and no hot water, only a cold tap and a copper for the washing. We had a range in the kitchen, which mother used to cook on and which kept the room warm. Our landlord was George White.

The front of the house faced north onto the backs of the houses in Eastern Road and some garages that were used for private car hire. When I was young there were horses kept there. Our own back yards faced south and my father kept chickens and grew vegetables there until Fyffes Bananas built a large warehouse which blocked out all our light and made the kitchen dark. My father was very cross about this and complained along with the others, but nothing was done. He painted a large board white and put it on top of the wall with the words 'Ancient Lights' written in large letters. That was his only way of protesting.

Not all the houses in Edwin Place were the same as ours. Some had basements and some had three storeys. We all had very nice gardens and took great pride in them. My father had a rose garden, with roses over the door and chrysanthemums in the autumn. During the summer months the gardens looked a picture. We had the same neighbours all the time we lived in Edwin Place, and I still keep in contact with some of the children whom I knew. We had lovely street parties in the yards with all of the children; everyone was very friendly.

At the east end, in Montague Place, there was a large wall belonging to Tamplin's brewery which all the children used for playing ball games against. I remember a pub in Montague Place. My mother would send me there to buy half a pint of stout for four pence. When it went up to fourpence ha'penny my mother refused to buy it any more.

We received notice that we would have to move and we were offered a house on the Manor Farm Estate, but my father said that was too far away from his work. He worked at the Royal Crescent Hotel as a kitchen porter and had to work funny hours and at weekends. Instead they offered us a flat in a new block to the south near the 'The Stag' pub. I don't think many of us objected to being moved, we just accepted what we were told. Most people were fascinated by the thought of having electric light and bathrooms, but many have moved back to the area from Manor Farm now that their families have grown up.

Kemp Town is not homely any more. That was comfort - that house in Edwin Place was lovely. This flat is very nice but blessed cold. We were never cold in Edwin Place. I've got central heating and everything but it doesn't come up to the standard of those little houses. If they'd put a bathroom and electricity in them they would have been lovely. It was such a pretty street.

Ivy Bone also lived in Edwin Place and remembers:

Our house was a two up, two down, with a couple of cellars underneath, a scullery out the back and a toilet across the yard. I can't remember our house being any bigger than the other houses in the street apart from the two cellars. Two houses had basements that they used for the family, but our cellars were too old and damp to be lived in. We used them in summer for keeping extra coal. The rooms were small, with just enough space in the two bedrooms for a big bed. There were five of us living in the house until my sister left to go into service at fourteen.

The rooms were lit by gas mantles. If mother was out when we returned home we were not allowed to touch the mantles; we had to sit in the dark. Not only were they too high to reach but they were very fragile and would crumble easily.

Our parlour was kept for special occasions, and I remember our next door neighbour's baby died very young and we had the little white coffin in it because they lived in all their rooms. In those days you always kept bodies in the front room or parlour, and my mum helped with the laying out of the body. Everyone came into our house to visit the baby, including the children.

We had lots of friends in Edwin Place and Eastern Road. On Good Friday we had a great big scaffold rope which we would turn, and both mothers and children would skip with it.

We were very trusting and never locked our doors. The insurance money was left on the table for the insurance man to come in and collect himself. The atmosphere was very warm and friendly. When one of us was really hard-up and we had holes in our shoes, the man at number two would mend them for us. He wasn't a cobbler by trade, but mended the neighbours' shoes to help them out.

Our landlady was a real 'so and so', she wouldn't repair the house. I can remember my mother wanting quite a few things doing. I think we had to do our own decorating. I can't imagine the landlady doing any.

My father worked for Davis & Sons in North Street as a furniture porter. He used to collect furniture from houses that were being cleared and also deliver it. It was a secure job despite the poor pay, and he worked there until he was seventy. My mother didn't work full-time outside the home, although when the new houses bought by Dad's firm were being made ready to move into she would help by scrubbing them out. My father's wages were about £2 a week and out of that the rent was eight shillings a week. Sometimes it was a terrible struggle to get by.

I went to St Mary's Church of England School by Upper Rock Gardens until I was eleven and then to Park Street School. Even if I'd passed the scholarship my Mum and Dad probably couldn't afford to send me to the Grammar School anyway. At my school we were taught how to make our own school uniform and I made my own gym slip skirt and blazer of which I was very proud.

I left school at fourteen. There wasn't much choice of jobs to go into. I wanted to be a hairdresser at first and my Mum took me for an interview to a shop, but you had to pay £50 to be trained and when I found this out I said I didn't want to do it. My Mum said that Dad could borrow the money off his boss, but I didn't want them to get into debt over me. What would happen if I didn't like it? So at first I did daily work cleaning houses, and I didn't like that. Then I went into service as did many girls. I went to work in Grand Avenue where I lived in as an In Between Maid, which meant I helped in the house in the morning and the kitchen in the afternoon, doing any jobs which were needed. I was only there for a matter of months as I didn't like it at all. I had to get up at 6 am and the other girls weren't very friendly. I then went to work for a couple in Lewes Crescent for five years and they were very nice. The Marshalls used to teach Siamese boys English at their house. After them I worked at St Dunstan's in St George's Road.

We were moved from Edwin Place to Cowfold Road. It was a two bedroomed, new house with an indoor toilet and bathroom, but my mother didn't want to move and she had a nervous breakdown soon afterwards because she wasn't happy living there. I think she felt very lonely and isolated and missed all her friends from Edwin Place. We never stayed long enough in Cowfold Road to get to know any of the neighbours, but no one in Cowfold Road was very friendly. Edwin Place was a nice environment and my Mum knew all the neighbours there, but we were given no choice about where we were to be moved to. We loved the friendliness of the community in Edwin Place.

E Kirby also recalls Edwin Place

I remember Edwin Place fondly. My parents lived there from 1917 to 1935. The houses had been condemned for about ten years, in spite of which they were still kept spotlessly clean. The neighbours were friendly without being in and out of each houses all the time, but were always there if anyone was ill or in trouble. My sister still sees her friends from Edwin Place, and we remember most of the neighbours' names.

Plan of Edwin Place

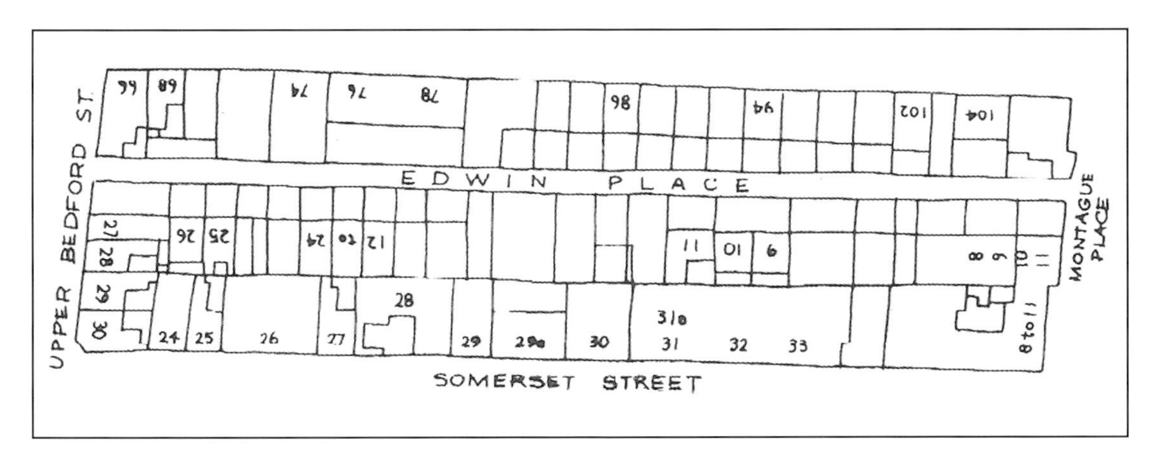

Carmine Amerena and family in Boss's Gardens, at 31 Edward Street c1914

Boss's Gardens

Boss's Gardens was a tiny lane off a narrow street, the third of the four lanes crammed into the 80 yards of steep slope between John Street and Mighell Street. Today it is under the American Express building.

Boss's Gardens was named after the gardens which were left untouched until the late 1850s between developments pressing in on all sides. The houses had small gardens at the front that gave a feeling of a little more spaciousness.

The Amerena family grew up there. Carmine, the head of the family, was occasionally one of the well-known trio of street musicians that Brightonians over a certain age will remember playing in North Street and East Street. A shopping trip on a Saturday was not complete until one had heard them. A painting of the them hangs in the Town Hall.

Jackie House recalls the Gardens:

My grandfather, Carmine Amerena, emigrated to England from Viggiano in southern Italy in the 1880s. Other Italian families also came from that area to England at that time. My grandfather was a violinist and he played with Mr Marcantonio and Mr Alexander, who played the violin and the harp. They played on the sea-front, on the beaches and on the paddle steamers that went to the Isle of Wight and beyond. They were the only three musicians that were given permission to play on the streets of Brighton, but my grandfather did not like doing this and it is the other two musicians that most people remember. Lyon & Hall, the music shop in Western Road, allowed them to copy their sheet music free of charge.

My grandfather initially settled in the St James's Street area with his English wife and family and later moved to Boss's Gardens. In 1906 he decided to emigrate with the family to America, possibly because his brother had decided to go. The fare to the US was £6. They left Southampton on the 'Philadelphia' and arrived at Ellis Island, New York, in October, but returned to England after a short time and settled in Brighton.

My mother Violetta was born in Boss's Gardens, a small row of houses running north from 31 Edward Street. She was only a few months old when they emigrated. The family returned to live in the same street when they came back from America.

There were other Italian families in the area but we did not live close to them, although my grandfather did socialise with a few friends. We did not speak Italian at home, which I regret because we could have been bilingual. I suppose the family wanted to integrate into the community, but they did keep their culture by attending St John the Baptist Catholic Church and School where all the children had a good education. The children always looked well-dressed and respectable. I remember going to look at Boss's Gardens just before it was demolished. They were empty then, so I could not go inside but they seemed very small and had gardens in front, which is possibly why they were called Boss's Gardens. My grandfather, Carmine, died in Brighton just at the end of the Second World War, aged 72. I can't remember much about the area but I do remember Cavendish Street with the ladies sitting outside with cloth caps and smoking pipes.

Roy Carmine Amerena remembers his grandfather and the Boys' Club:

After my grandparents returned from America they did not stay long in Boss's Gardens but moved to Devonshire Street. At the bottom of that road, on Edward Street, was the Brighton Boys' Club, which was important to me when growing up. It was a wonderful establishment that did an awful lot for the youngsters of Brighton, especially those who were rather hard up or came from large families.

There were three clubs - one for the under thirteens, a junior club and a senior club for those over fifteen. They were open to every boy who paid the membership fee, but I think that was only pennies. It was run by the National Association of Boys' Clubs through a Warden called Mr Tyrer, plus a Secretary who played an important part. The Club was supported by charities, and we also raised our own finances by holding jumble sales, boxing matches and support from boys' parents. I first went to the Club when I was about 13.

There was a gymnasium, billiard tables and darts. You were also encouraged to enjoy a game of chess and there was a successful table tennis team. It had a good carpentry shop where boys were taught woodworking skills. The teacher was a very good man, but things could get out of hand and on one occasion a boy threw a chisel right across the room. Such behaviour could lead to you being expelled from the Club.

There were a lot of boys from poor homes and I believe some boys who had got into trouble with the law. Instead of being sent to a Remand Home there was an undertaking that they would attend the Boys' Club. The warden would have to keep a close eye on them and the boys were obliged to attend. There they would meet boys with a different points of view and they wouldn't be able to dominate a given situation. They had to respect the older boys; if not they were in real trouble - not from the Warden - but the boys themselves. It was an organisation where boys helped other boys, under supervision.

My grandfather Carmine was a very accomplished musician and he used to allow me to play on his harp. At one time he played the violin on paddle steamers, but being in a very bad storm once he vowed never to go to sea again, and he didn't. For leisure he would go shooting because I remember there were two guns and a bag behind the door of his house. He was a very wise man but had difficulty reading English and my grandmother, who was English, always read to him. During the war he was interned because he was still an Italian citizen, even though he was in his late sixties and had a son and grandson fighting for England. My grandmother used to go and visit him every week.

In the 1930s fewer houses were pulled down around Devonshire Street than happened further down the hill towards the Steine, but I clearly remember the start of the demolition in our area when I was about twelve. It must have been a great wrench when people were moved from their homes. It needed doing, but it upset the spirit and emotion of the people who lived there. When people were given new houses some thought they were in a palace, but others were less happy. The young people could cope but the older people sometimes could not.

Poverty was widespread in the area, and it is a blessing that we have moved on from that, but I don't think people are necessarily happier with more material things. The people in those areas made their own enjoyment. We were very creative and full of spirit and generally self-supporting. It gave people confidence and character and the spirit was wonderful, but I am surprised how some people managed to survive their extreme poverty.

Later I was involved in developing Edward Street and under 'The Globe' pub, opposite Dorset Gardens, we found a tunnel that was blocked with bricks and cement. It ran under Edward Street, along Dorset Gardens and came out where the Aquarium is. The story was that it was originally used for smuggling. We also discovered two wells there under large paving stones and I dropped a stone in to see how deep it was and decided the water level was about that of Grand Parade. Afterwards we had to fill them in with debris and cement.

Roger Amerena recalls his great-grandfather:

My great-grandfather came to England at the age of sixteen in 1889. He came from a very small and poor village in southern Italy that had been devastated by a great earthquake around 1875. Though small, Viggiano was famous for its musicians, particularly its harpists. Carmine himself played the harp in addition to the violin. When not playing he sold fruit.

He married a girl from Suffolk named Maud and they had six children. When they emigrated they took with them Mr Alexander and M Marcantonio, who also came from the village of Viggiano.

There are still about twenty Amerenas in Brighton, who have made a sizeable contribution to the town since 1889.

Hayllar's Cottages

Unlike the rest of Backyard Brighton, Hayllar's cottages were in the heart of the Old Town and seem to have been erected quite late for Old Town developments, in the 1840s.

Hayllar's Cottages were originally called Hayllar's Court. In the 1851 Census, 18 Middle Street was the home of Daniel Hayllar, age 60, a carpenter, and his family. It is likely that the Hayllar family built the cottages on their garden, hence the name, as there was little planning control and a great demand for housing at that time. The ten cottages were very small and probably only had one room on each floor. The occupants in 1851 included four fishermen, two watermen and a fishmonger.

From the 1860s to the 1920s the Fillis family occupied 18 Middle Street. William Fillis was a tailor employing one boy. His wife Esther was a dressmaker employing two girls. Three of the four daughters became dressmakers. Ada Fillis, born in 1861, was still listed as a dressmaker at 18 Middle Street in a 1920 Street Directory.

Alistair Tapsell recalls the remains of the Cottages:

I remember living at 18 Middle Street during World War Two. It was a cottage where there was a nice garden at the back where I used to play with my twin brother. The garden had been the site of ten cottages called Hayller's Cottages, and in the early days we had had a much longer garden with a lane right through to West Street where Willow Cottages had been.

These old cottages were demolished in 1936 and all one could see when I was there was the outline of masonry, wooden horizontal timbers set in the wall and slots above for joists. My father, trying to make a proper garden, had dug up big piles of rubble and stones that he piled into raised beds on either side. In the passage of time we lost the end of the garden where we had kept chickens and ducks as we only rented this part from the Council at a peppercorn rent until they needed it.

The cottages must have been very close together because our garden wasn't all that wide. I would think that they were one up and one down, and I can't imagine that there was room for a toilet inside the cottage. There were still remnants of drains left from the cottages and so we had a rat problem. Originally they may have been fishermen's cottages because when my father was excavating he found a pile of fish innards.

The entrance to Hayller's Cottages was through a passage between 18 and 19 Middle Street. The construction of 18 Middle Street was strange. You couldn't have pulled down number 18 without making number 19 unusable because there was a tied wall

opposite top: Hayllar's Cottages looking west 1935

opposite bottom: the Cottages looking east, with the entrance from Middle Street

over the top of the passageway. Once you took the render off the front of the house you found strange looking tiles and ship's timbers and boards behind where you could see peg marks. I've seen similar construction elsewhere in the world where you get these long low passages opening out into another community behind.

A seamstress at some point may have used our house because in one area underneath the floor we found loads of needles and bits and pieces of material.

From Alderman Dutton Briant

22 Marlborough Place
Brighton
6 December 1937

Dear Sir

Re: 1-5 Hayllar's Cottages

It appears that on the 25th July 1935, the Council by resolution decided to acquire the above property under a Compulsory Purchase Order for the clearance of the site as a slum area. This was subject of an Enquiry held by the Ministry of Health on the 4th December 1935, and on the 5th June 1936 Notice To Treat was served on the owners. After prolonged negotiations in March of this year the property was eventually purchased by the Corporation at the sum of £575. In September of this year the Corporation intimated to the late owner's agent that they had no immediate use for this site, and would be prepared to resell it, and as a result of negotiations the property was offered to the previous owner for the sum of £1100.

These facts appear to be completely substantiated by correspondence which has been handed to me. I cannot understand how the Corporation came to purchase these premises for demolition at the price of £575 and expect in six months' time to resell the bare site to the same owners for the sum of £1100. Will you kindly supply me with the reason for this site being dealt with in this manner.

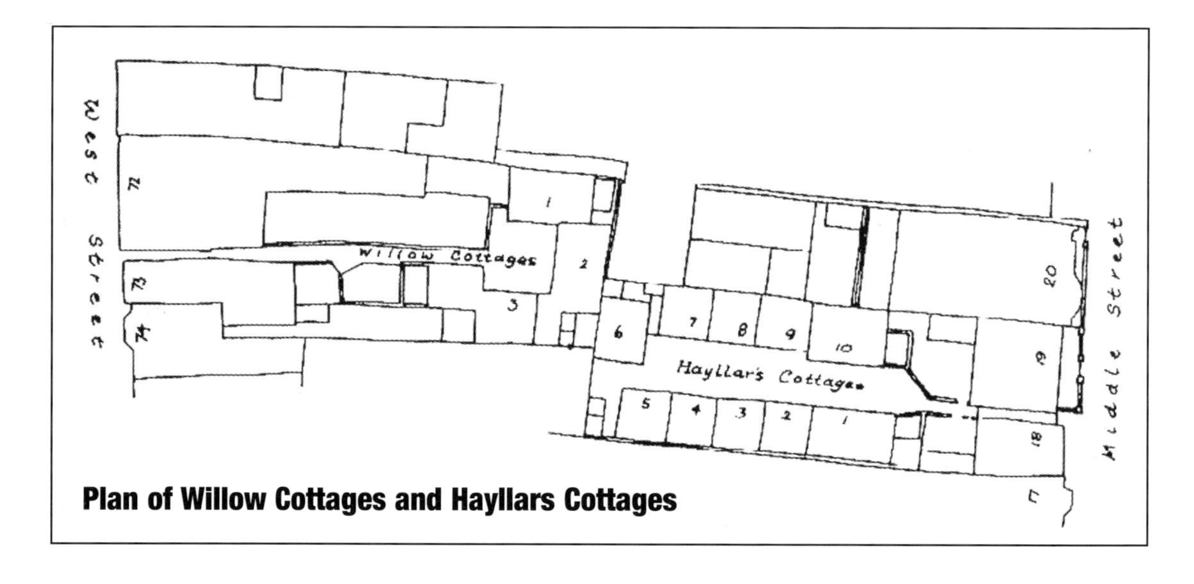

Plan of Willow Cottages and Hayllars Cottages

Artillery Street

Artillery Street lay behind the Grand Hotel and is today under the lower level car park at Churchill Square. Dating from the 1850s, originally called Suffolk Place, it was infill between the earlier developments of Cannon Street and Russell Street.

Pat Sprinthall describes her life there:

I lived in a small terraced house in Artillery Street. I felt a bit ashamed of the address when we first moved there as we had previously lived in King's Road. My mother was very pleased when she first found the house as it was newly decorated, but we soon found it was 'buggy'.

I had a marvellous childhood. I and my sister attended the Band of Hope at Holy Trinity Church in Ship Street. We did not know what it was for, and have since learned it was something to do with not drinking. We were in the Brownies, and with them had to attend Sunday School. I did not want to go but it was lovely if you were the one allowed to carry the flag.

We used to travel all over the town alone from as young as five, spending whole days on the beach and ages in the sea. We would play in the fishermen's boats because I knew them all from living in King's Road, where we had a tunnel from the basement through to the beach arches.

On Fridays the family would go to the Hippodrome, up in the Gods, and then to 'The Gloucester' pub where they had a children's room. I and my sister used to wait for autographs outside the Hippodrome. We also went to the children's programmes at the Prince's Cinema at the top of North Street and the Academy in West Street. On Bonfire Night there were big bonfires on the beach with fireworks. I can still smell that now. It was so exciting. Everyone was neighbourly in Artillery Street and children seemed so much safer in those days.

I did well at school and passed the scholarship exam to go to Varndean. In fact I almost passed to go to the High School. I was the only one from my school to do that, but I failed the oral exam. I expect I did not speak nicely enough for them.

We received a grant of £10 for expenses at Varndean, which I loved for the first year. I did not mind not having any good friends with me. I was in the top class and studied French and Latin. During the War I began to lose interest, and when most of my friends started work I got restless. My parents had signed an undertaking that I would stay at school until sixteen, but things were not so strict during the War and I left early to go to work at a jeweller's in King's Road, threading beads all day. After two weeks I had had enough and went to work in a shoe shop. Later I was directed into work on radio parts at the old ice rink, S S Brighton, in West Street, and then on the buses.

I don't think we were poor. We were probably better off than many. We always ate well and I had some nice clothes. Some streets were poor. Cannon Street seemed poorer and the children more ragged. Other streets like Grenville Place seemed to be wealthier.

Mrs Goodwin also has good memories of the street:

We lived at 12 Artillery Street. There was always so much to do there. You could go to the bottom of the road and you were on the beach. There was the Palladium cinema round the corner, the Ice Rink in West Street and the shops in Western Road. There was a pie man at the corner of Air Street by the Clock Tower who had a funny little black oven on wheels and would heat the pies for you. We would go winkle picking at Black Rock and Mum would boil them. They were horrible, little screaming things. We would then sell them at thruppence for a half pint.

We would walk to Stanmer Park and pick bluebells and primroses, tie them on a stick and walk back and sell them on Western Road. From houses that had been bombed we would collect wood, chop it up and sell it in little bundles. We were always doing something, and my Mum was pleased that we earned a few pence. They were hard working days for children but it was fun, because you were finding out things and making a little money too.

Another place we went to was 'The Scratch', the nickname for the 'Arcadia' in Lewes Road. You could get in there for sixpence or a shilling. It had a long foyer and all the Mums would leave their pushchairs there whilst they were watching the picture. I would have to keep going out to check on the kids.

Quite a few men in the street worked at Tamplin's Brewery. and because of the brewery there was always a lot of coming and going, with lorries galore. But at weekends it was quieter and we could play out there.

The houses in Artillery Street were tall, dim and smelly. Most of them were owned by private landlords and were reasonable to live in and cheap. Hardly any of the electricity worked because of the spongy walls. When you put on a switch you were liable to get a shock. It is a shame they are not there any more. Although they were slums they were happy places. You could go out and leave your front and back door open and nobody would go in. If anyone did call in it was to say 'Can I help you' or 'I've got the kettle on'. The kids did have scraps, but it did not boil into anything with the neighbours. I cannot believe all that understanding of years past has just gone.

Artillery Street was fun to live in. It is a shame to have lost touch with all those people.

Kathleen Davis remembers Christmas in Artillery Street:

We had a three storey house with a ground floor sitting room, a back room, an outside lavatory but with running water inside. If the houses had kept going a bit longer they would have modernised them and would be fit for a family today.

End Piece

These tales of life lived on the edge of society speak to us across the years for their warmth, humanity and sense of uprightness. The people talk movingly of the difficulties, but also the many pleasures, of life in Backyard Brighton. Though separated from us by an astonishing degree of poverty as well as time, we can still relate to the basic needs and aspirations they express, and even the gentle snobberies of street on street.

The stories bring to life for us a busy and socially content group of Brightonians, and are not simply a recitation of the awful material conditions they struggled so hard to overcome. For it is not just the buildings but the communities that have gone, along with so many of the amiable folk pastimes. Not everyone had extended families, but everyone had neighbours. The demolition of a neighbourhood was also the destruction of a complex social support system. People felt they belonged to their area of the town - to that small collection of streets around their home - and everyone knew where that area began and ended.

Such close-knit groupings probably could not have survived the huge social changes of the last fifty years - the mobility of families, increased car ownership, the electronic life style of easy communication, the television entertainment culture - but their passing is still something to regret. So much of present day political discourse refers to 'community', but these were real communities, with bonds much stronger than we can have today because they were born of shared misfortune and fixed, close family ties.

It is hard for us at this distance in time to form a balanced judgment on the buildings themselves or the actions of the authorities. Many of the cunning techniques of restoration that we take for granted today were not available in the thirties, forties and fifties of the last century. The small scale of the houses would not now be such cause for condemnation, with today's nuclear families replacing the crush stemming from yearly offspring.

Nevertheless the injustice of the compensation regime and the steely determination of the Council and its officers still give cause for discomfort. It seems undeniable that if it had been possible to save the buildings the town would have a much greater character than it has today. Small pockets of such housing that somehow escaped the swathe of destruction show us that. To stand in Frederick Gardens, off North Road, or Queen's Place near the Level, is to mourn the huge losses. Today we have only these photos to see that other, older Brighton.

Afterword : Kingswood Flats

Kingswood Flats left

Renee Kelly and Mary Banks were rehoused from Cavendish Street into the Kingswood flats, built in 1938 on the site of Nelson Place and the Primitive Methodist chapel in Sussex Street.

Renee and Mary relate how their housing conditions improved, although poverty persisted:

They had already demolished some of the area and were building the Milner and Kingswood flats, when mum went down to the offices and asked about moving there. She only had her name down for two weeks and they gave her a flat. Mr Holt, the Housing Manager, took her round and she had the choice of four flats. They were all new then and she picked number 54. The rent was 12/6d per week. Our dad had to put some furniture in a pram to bring it down the hill. It was a two bed room flat, but there were three bed roomed flats in the turrets and possibly one four bed room flat. There were bedsits for the old people on the ground floor. When it rained they'd put out all their Aspidistras and other big plants.
The flats were actually maisonettes except for the ground floor. There was a lounge with a big, black grate with an oven on top and a shelf. We had a stove in the kitchen but you could cook on the grate if you wanted to. Our mum used to clean that grate with black lead, she was really house proud. She would also clean her outside balcony every day on her hands and knees. Upstairs there were two bedrooms with fireplaces, and a bathroom.

There was a refuse chute, one to every four flats. You had to wrap your refuse up in newspaper and put it down the chute and every week the dustmen would come and take this great big bin out. I felt sorry for the people downstairs because they got the smells. My mum also complained about the smells because the hatch was near our front window and some people didn't wrap their refuse. After the refuse had been collected she would light a newspaper and push it down the hatch to 'clean it'. The smoke would billow out, I don't know what the people downstairs thought. The chutes are now bolted shut. There was also a fire escape outside each flat but they were also taken away. It was a hoop and a pulley and you had to lower yourself to the ground.

The flats got a bad name but I bet you that 99% of the people that lived there were spotless. The only reason that they got a bad name was that some of them were barrow boys and their names and addresses would go in the Argus when they were fined for illegal trading. Some of them didn't even live in the flats but they'd give an address there. When we moved into the flats there would be be rows of people leaning over the balconies and talking. All the kiddies played together.

We watched the streets above us - Claremont Street & John Street - being pulled down and we called that area 'The Dumps'. It may be another reason why people called this a slummy place to live. Nelson Street was already knocked down when we moved in and we just had the footings of the old houses. Nothing was done during the war, so they remained like that. We used to have fun over there right up as far as the stables behind where the new Carlton Hill school was, in front of the crèche. We still call that street Nelson Street today although it is now known as John Street. The small road in front of the flats is still called Nelson Row.

There were originally bike sheds in the turrets of the flats. Each flat was allocated its own space and had their own key. Our dad worked for the Gas Board and he kept his tools in there. During the war the bike sheds were knocked through to make a big space and when the bombing was really bad everyone had their mattresses down there and we all slept there. After the war all these areas were made into additional flats.

Everyone was poor but we were all in the same boat, nobody had anything. The only robberies there were was when the gas meters were broken into but sometimes the tenants had done it themselves. Mum used to do her washing on a Monday and if she had soapy water left when she'd finished she would take it in a bucket to a neighbour. Sometimes neighbours would knock at the door and ask if she had any water left. During the war soap was rationed and it cost money to heat the water.

When mum went to work during the war she'd always leave the key in the door on a bit of string so that we could get in when we returned home from school. At night she'd just hang the key over the latch. Nobody ever came up to the flats, only people who lived there.

We've got central heating and double-glazing now and I've had a new kitchen but I've still got my original bath. People used to stay in the flats for years and years, but nowadays everything is fleeting, they come, they go, it's all transient. There's one or two I know but not like years ago when we were kids together when it had a strong community spirit. When girls married they still lived near their mums and one time we both lived here in flats at the same time as our parents. We were always down at our parents' flat, so we got to know who was moving and we got in first.

HAIR
CUTTING
&
SHAVING

Interviews

As a result of articles published in the Evening Argus, Brighton & Hove Gazette and broadcasts on Radio Sussex people who knew and lived in the streets depicted here have written or spoken about their memories of the places where they grew up.

The interviews conducted by Jacqueline Pollard, and the written accounts, provide a close focus view of people's lives in the 1930s and '40s. In many cases they have detailed their experiences through their eyes as children.

The contrast with our expectations of life today is dramatic. The inhabitants of these streets were united by poverty, so they built up strong support networks within the community to help them survive the rigours of their lives.

Many thanks to the following people who contrbuted so much to Backyard Brighton:

Roger Amerena, Roy Carmine Amerena, Georgina Attrell, Mary Banks, Dorothy Betteridge, Ivy Bone, Benjamin Bowman, L Boyle, Victor Cox, Kathleen Davis, Dorothy Farrell, Bernard Goldberg, Mrs Goodwin, Tom Gower, W Holmes, Margaret Hamon, Jackie House, Renee Kelly, E Kirby, A Lambert, Bert Nelson, Rose, Winnie and Edie; L Scarborough, Amelia Scholey, Pat Sprinthall, Gladys Stenning, Charlotte Storrey, Alistair Tapsell, Henry Tullett, Ernest Whittington, Charles Yeates

Without them this book would not exist.

Opposite: North Street Cottages, at 26 Meeting House Lane 1935

Acknowledgements

'Backyard Brighton: new memories, reflections and photographs' is a re-edited version of 'Backyard Brighton' (1988) and includes a new Foreword, Introduction, Preface, interviews and photographs.

The first edition and two subsequent reprints of Backyard Brighton were published by the Lewis Cohen Urban Studies Centre at Brighton Polytechnic, now the University of Brighton; and QueenSpark Books, who provided the funding.

Historical research: Jacqueline Pollard
Interviews: © Jacqueline Pollard
Design and editing: Selma Montford
Editing, additional text and research: Derek Burns
Design consultant: Simon Montgomery

Photographs
Photographic research: Jacqueline Pollard
Many of the photographs are reproduced with the kind permission of the Royal Pavilion, Libraries and Museums (Brighton & Hove)
Some of the photographs are reproduced from the J S Gray collection with the kind permission of the Regency Society of Brighton & Hove
Chris Horlock loaned some of the photographs
Roger Amerena loaned the photograph of his family
Photographs have been reproduced with the assistance of Duncan McNeill and Bob Seago

Freehand drawn maps: © Lavender Jones
Teaching and technical support: Computer Box
Readers: Christine Davies and Moira Monteith
Typing: Alice Elliott

References: Underdog Brighton, Rocky Hill, Iconoclast Press 1991. Georgian Brighton, S Berry, Phillimore & Co 2003. Living Back to Back, C Upton, Phillimore & Co 2005. The Encyclopædia of Brighton, Timothy Calder, East Sussex County Libraries 1990. Map: New Ordnance Atlas of Brighton 1882.

Printed by Delta Press, Unit 1, Industrial House, Conway Street, Hove BN3 3LW

Published 2007 by Brighton Books Publishing ISBN 978-1-901454-10-9
Partners: Jacqueline Pollard and Selma Montford

10 Clermont Road Brighton BN1 6SG

phone: 01273-509209 fax: 01273-502018 email: info@brightonbooks.co.uk

website: www.brightonbooks.co.uk   blog: http://brightonbooks.wordpress.com